"Did I Really Do My Hair for *This*?"

Stephanie Goldman

Also Released by Sakura Publishing

When Heaven Calls

Fortino

Touretties

Lost Evidents

Dump Your Problems!

The Legend of Willow Springs Farm

Stricken Yet Crowned

"Did I Really Do My Hair for This?"

Stephanie Goldman

To my best friends,
Without you there would be no good
stories to tell.
To all the girls out there still
searching for "Mr. Right,"
Keep getting back up and dusting
yourself off- he's on his way.

Table of Contents

"You Really Should Write a Book One Day!"

So, I have always thought I could write a very entertaining book, but my fear of pissing people off, losing all my friends, and the world knowing what I really think has kept me shut tighter than a girl scout on Charlie Sheen's doorstep. However, I have recently discovered that some former friends have written a few really great blogs, and those don't offend me—so I thought I'd give it a shot. I have changed some of the details in the following stories, like names, dates, and places, to protect the identities of those involved. That way, I'll still have some friends left. Some of the thoughts in this book I would never express out loud. But isn't that what writing is for: to hide behind the shield of a book cover?

Let's begin with what I learned yesterday in preparation to meet some friends at a birthday party:

> **Never put on makeup, do your hair, or pick out an outfit while intoxicated, ladies!**

A toddy (or two) to loosen up before a big date or event is fine, but don't hit the bong or shoot the tequila until you are ready to hit the door. Unless the "Lady Gaga Meets Amanda Winehouse (*God rest her junkie soul*) on a 'Girls Only' Margarita Night at the Local Best Western Bar" is the look you are going for. You may have thought you just pulled off the Victoria's Secret "tousled hair and bedroom eyes" look in record time, but you really just look as fucked up as you feel the morning after said girls' night out.

Part One

The Beginning of the End

I am not quite sure exactly when my boy craziness started. My first memory is from Kindergarten. I would position myself daily within the line of sight of my first crush, Daniel. I would stare at him all day, until he was moved to the other side of the room (He told his mother that the girl across from him was always "blinking" at him). Or maybe it all began when I begged my mother to take a little boy named David to the circus with us in first grade. I can't say for sure, but my first real experience with excess in the boy department was in third grade.

His name was Jamey, and I pined over him daily. He unfortunately was "dating" my best friend Bree. This was also my first experience with "frenemies" (I really wish we'd had all these sayings like "frenemies" and "bromance" when I was young. It would have made so much easier the explanations to my New Kids on the Block diary). Back to the point, "dating" in third grade consisted of playing on the same kickball team, sitting within the same vicinity at the lunch table, and possibly sneaking off to play tether ball together, if you were *really* serious. Jamey was a soccer goalie. I thought his fluorescent shirt was ugly, so I told him he was gay.

Now, in third grade, I had no idea what "gay" was. I thought you were gay if you wore bright colors and changed the shoelaces of your Keds weekly. Maybe, that's why my preference of color palette has always leaned toward neutrals? Anyway, of course, the little brat told on me, and I had to sit inside during recess for a week. My mother told me not to talk to Jamey anymore, but that did not deter me.

Fast forward to summer vacation. Just as with every summer of my life up until I moved away permanently when I was eighteen, I had been with my family on our farm outside of Nashville,

Tennessee. We had a large horse barn with an attached rec room. I would spend the humid afternoons in there. The room just so happened to have a phone, but parents are too nosy. Why do they demand to know who you are calling when you are hiding under the covers on the top bunk bed? Doesn't every nine year-old girl deserve some privacy? My parents' overbearing behavior forced me to sneak off to the rec room to call Jamey. I didn't think anything of it. I just wanted to chit chat, ask how his summer was going, see if he knew what teacher he had in the fall for fourth grade (I had submitted my written request that we be placed in the same class back in May).

Well, I was a bit taken aback when his mother answered the phone. She was not happy. Was it the fact that the girl that had called her son "gay" was now calling him on the phone? Or was she pissed off about the long distance charges? Who knows! All I knew was how lucky I was that she did not tell my mom that Jamey and I would not be in the same class ever again. Nor did he ever speak to me all the way through eighth grade.

> **What I should have taken away from this experience is that, if he doesn't come to or answer the phone, then he probably is not interested—whether he is nine or twenty-nine. It doesn't matter.**

So, Jamey, if you happen to be reading this: CALL ME!!!

Don't Tell Mom the Babysitter's Drunk

I learned a lot of things at an inappropriately young age. My best friend from the fourth grade taught me how to give a hand-job to a banana while we were sitting on the back pew in Chapel. I learned what a blow-job was when my fifth grade art class mocked me for befriending a boy unfortunately named "B.J." (I cringe to think that my two young nieces might know even half of what I knew at their age. I'm sure my sixteen year-old, homosexual nephew is the potential culprit: he already ruined Santa and the Easter Bunny for his younger cousins, although, he still gets a bit skittish when anyone mentions the Tooth Fairy, or fairies of any kind, for that matter).

However, when I was in the sixth grade and at the ripe age of twelve, I learned my most valuable lesson from a babysitter, for whom my parents apparently forgot to check the references.

> ### Never Mix Dark and Light Liquor.

Now, when my new, seventeen year-old babysitter showed up, she seemed innocent enough. My parents told her she could take me for ice cream if I finished all of my homework. She got all the emergency numbers and seemed responsible enough for a girl that punctuated every sentence with "dude." Her inability to speak with correct grammar noted, I thought she'd be an easy mark. I had fooled much smarter babysitters into thinking I was an angel. At twelve, I didn't think I needed a chaperone for anything. But, after one too many toaster fires and prank calls telling the police I was giving birth in a bathroom stall at the local gas station, I couldn't really blame my parents for wanting to keep me in line and out of juvie.

Before I even had a chance to open my Trapper Keeper and start my homework, the babysitter announced we were going for a ride and asked me where my car seat was. I thought, ***Bitch, just because I'm shorter than you* does not mean I need a car seat—and I don't even want to be seen *in your 1984 SAAB!*** After a short ride, we pulled up to what sure as hell did not look anything like a Baskin Robbins. This punk had dragged me to a party she wasn't even invited to! I mean, she couldn't even go inside! I sat in the car for three hours while she and her friends drank whatever they could find out of the near-empty liquor bottles sitting in the driveway. She shot-gunned a few beers and moved on to shooting vodka (From this point, I thought shooting vodka was okay, until I tried it in college. My Noxzema astringent tasted better). After a few vodka shots, someone showed up with a half-empty bottle of Jack Daniels. This girl chugged the whole thing! I was in awe.

At this moment, the belligerent babysitter was my new idol. I wanted to be just like her, fake nose ring and all. From the passenger's seat, she babbled about getting ice cream, while the only sober person with a driver's license drove us home in her car. I prayed that we wouldn't get pulled over, and that my parents were just dumb enough to let her babysit again.

I went to bed that night dreaming of all the fun we would have. She could teach me about boys and how to act slutty without actually having to be a slut (She would tell me that's how she got her college boyfriend). I was in the middle of dreaming up my own older boyfriend, when he suddenly threw a drink in my face—which felt a bit too real. I wasn't dreaming anymore, but instead I abruptly woke up to a real life fucking nightmare. This drunken excuse of a role model had stumbled into my bedroom, mistaking it for the bathroom, and puked on me. **Puked on me!**

I do not "do" any kind of gross bodily liquid; I have already decided not to have children because I just cannot handle spit up and shit of any kind. Once I had realized that this girl had actually thrown up on me, my OCD took over and I immediately ran to the shower. After three showers, which included scrubbing with Cascade dish soap and hydrogen peroxide, I found the babysitter in the downstairs bathroom. At least the bitch had eventually made it to the right place. She was rocking back and forth in front of the toilet, mumbling something about how I was so rude to her and that she should double her rate.

I told her I wouldn't tell my parents—but I would tell hers. I took her cell phone and dialed her mom. I told the babysitter's unfit mother to come pick up her daughter ASAP because she just puked on a twelve year-old, or I was going to call DCS. After the babysitter's cracked-out mom and boyfriend picked her up and physically carried her away, I had to do damage control. My bedroom was soaked in vomit, and I just knew my parents would pull the "well, you should have called us when you knew she was drinking" card. How was I supposed to know the girl couldn't handle her alcohol?

Well, that bitch never took me for mine. I proceeded to trash my comforter and eat too much ice cream out of the fridge. I crawled into my parent's bed and waited for their return. When they got home, they were horrified to learn that the babysitter had given me too much ice cream, which in turn gave me a horrible stomachache, and she'd had the nerve to run from the house, screaming like a mad woman when I predictably got sick! Of course I was going to blame it on the bitch.

> **Besides learning that you don't mix dark and light, I learned a few other things, too. I can spin anything my way. Oh, and that old saying, "Beer before liquor, never been sicker; liquor before beer, you're in the clear," has never been truer.**

First Kiss

The summer before I started high school, I was still the only one of my friends that had not kissed a boy. Most of them had kissed a boy by sixth grade and had already moved on to giving hand-jobs and getting fingered in the back row of school assemblies. It was mostly my own fault that I had not been kissed yet.

My high anxiety had always caused me to be my own worst enemy. I would obsess about what to do with my tongue and for how long and in what motion. I would over-analyze the different hand placements I could go with. Do I place them on his back? Or, clutch his hair Harlequin style? Or, should I try to put my hand down his pants and just go for the grab, or is that too slutty? I would lay awake at night worrying myself to death about how I would make this happen. While I was practicing giving tongue to my pillow, all my friends had moved on to the real thing, and no boys at my junior high wanted to kiss the prude.

I spent all summer searching for other options to be my first kiss. The Fourth of July came and went. I thought that surely I could find some pre-pubescent boy to kiss me during some fireworks. After all, isn't that the American Dream? No such fucking luck. I was getting very worried that I would start high school without being kissed, which would potentially ruin my whole life. I wouldn't have another chance until college! I was beginning to have nightmares about dying an old, virgin maid (I should have probably gotten a good vibrator right then).

Labor Day weekend arrived, and I was starting ninth grade in less than a week. I decided that I either had to kiss someone in the next forty-eight hours or demand that I be home-schooled. So, I went to the place that was my last hope for

"Did I Really Do My Hair for This?" **9**

finding any viable, young males to kiss me; I hit the county fair. Southern California county fairs are pretty similar to what county fairs are in other parts of the country—except, instead of tractor pulls, there were drop-top hydraulic car shows, and the carnies were a bit better-looking. Anyway, I went with a girl that lived in my neighborhood named Jackie. Jackie was sixteen, could drive, and was a slut. I figured she would take me right to where the boys were. And, she did.

She was obsessed with a junior that went to a school a few cities away. He looked like he hadn't showered in weeks, and that's what Jackie found attractive about him. I called him "Stanky." He thought I was a smart-ass little kid, but he had this hot friend, Grady, that thought I was cute. It helped that Jackie and Stanky didn't laugh when I lied and told Grady I was sixteen (Women always lie about their age. My mom had been thirty-nine for as long as I could remember). I didn't see any harm with fudging my age by two years. I even told him an elaborate story about how my brand new convertible Mustang was in the shop getting twenty-two-inch rims. I stuck to Grady like white on rice. I told him about my (imaginary) college boyfriend, so I would seem mature. I watched him play skee ball for hours and decided that I was going to kiss this guy if I had to knock him out with one of them.

After the fair, Stanky invited us to an after-party at his house. His parents were out of town and, from what I had read in US Weekly, I knew that all after-parties had booze, drugs, sex, and sometimes an impromptu performance by a rapper. I told my parents I was having a slumber party at Jackie's, and then I was all set up to get this thing done! Well, the "after-party" turned out to be just the four of us. Once Jackie left to give Stanky a blow-job in his bedroom, it was just

Grady and me on the couch. I was about to break out in a cold sweat. After a few minutes of awkward silence, he started massaging my breasts through my Guess Jeans top. This was skipping a few steps, but, whatever. I have never been one to do things in order. Finally, Grady leaned in and put his tongue in my mouth. This was awesome! In a matter of three minutes, I had gone from a fourteen year-old that had never been kissed to a pretend sixteen year-old approaching second base.

The kiss was okay. To this day, the taste of cigarettes and O'Doul's non-alcoholic beer remind me of that night. I even let him feel me up under my top, but over the bra, for a bit. I had a lot of ground to make up, but I grew bored quickly. I'd never had much of an attention span. I went home that night on cloud nine. I somehow decided that Grady was my new boyfriend without consulting him first. All of my junior high friends became couples once they kissed. That must have been how it worked in high school. I had already worked out my stories for the next two years on how I would avoid the age subject with Grady. I would just throw myself down the stairs every few months and say I totaled my car again; a few bumps and bruises would explain why I had no car and my parents took my driver's license away. Whoops!

We had exchanged numbers, and I called him incessantly. I even sent cute little "I miss U" messages to his pager using numbers. Grady could rarely ever hang out, though. He was always very busy with football practice and working on his car. He did promise to take me to the Homecoming dance at my school. I had intentionally made friends with juniors so he would believe my whole charade. I actually let them use my pool and bought them lunch in exchange for them corroborating my story. Homecoming came, and I was ready to impress with my boyfriend from another school. I had my hair extensions in and was looking hot (I was all over the hair extension thing long before J-Lo ever got off that block). I waited for what I had anticipated to be the best night of my life. It was what I considered to be our second date/one-month anniversary. I was going to catch up with everyone else and slide into third base. It seemed like I always had catching up in the sexual department, although I had lapped everyone else by the time I actually did turn 16. I waited for hours after Grady was supposed to pick me up, but he wasn't just extremely and unfashionably late: he never showed.

I had been stood up! I was furious and humiliated. He would not answer my calls and didn't even have the balls to make up an excuse. I tried sending a numerical "I hate U" to his pager, but the number had been disconnected. The next day, his phone number had been changed, too. I was devastated. I bitched it out to Jackie when she picked me up for school Monday morning. She kind of smirked and said, "Steph, I don't think you will be hearing from Grady again, ever." The look on her face said that she wasn't telling me something. After bribing her for information by promising to let her do some nude sunbathing in my very private backyard after school, she finally told me the truth. The little bastard was thirteen years-old! He had lied about his age, too! When he tried to steal his dad's car to take me to Homecoming, his parents grounded him. I didn't even get grounded anymore! The manipulator had been manipulated.

I never saw Grady again until years later, when he showed up on a local sex offender website. Apparently, he would have been better off sticking with older women.

Brace Yourself

Since I was the last one of my friends to kiss a boy, I had a lot of ground to cover—and fast. By sixteen, I still had only just gotten past first base. My friends were already comparing blow job techniques with each other in gym class. I wanted to know the correct fellatio protocol, too. I hate not doing something the right way. If it's not done right, then I don't want to waste my time, and I'll find someone that will get it done correctly. I couldn't hire a stand-in to give blow jobs for me, could I? Everyone else in high school was fumbling around, experimenting, and "discovering" their sexuality with a partner that was just as inexperienced as they were. What was the use in that? I tried make-out sessions with a few boys, but they knew less than I did. I needed to be taught correctly the first time.

I convinced myself that I could make up for what I lacked in looks with sexual experience and know-how. Maybe even learn a few special tricks. It wasn't until a few years later when I noticed that the girls I used to hang out with were now buying diapers, instead of the condoms they should have been stockpiling, that I realized something very important. Thinking that you need to sleep with as many people as you can only gets you a one-way ticket to the last round of *Sixteen and Pregnant* auditions. Thank goodness I was able to see the light and chart the correct path.

> **It's about quality, not quantity. That tidbit works for everything in life— everything!**

Most of the guys I write about I have not slept with. Having sex with only a few carefully selected partners is way better than letting every frat guy from here to Mississippi get it in. At this time, I was the last sixteen year-old virgin in Orange County. That, in and of itself, should have awarded me some kind of college scholarship. Maybe the nose job did set me back in the race to be normal in the quintessential OC, but I was still more grounded than most girls at my school.

But, I still had a mission to complete. After I had wasted my previous years of high school letting boys fumble with my bra and slobbering all over my face, I went away for the summer looking for a more educational experience. While spending the summer at my family's farm in Tennessee, I met a cute nineteen year-old farm boy named Brandon. He was big and strong and starting his second year at the local community college. He was working at another farm nearby, and he definitely had the "sexy tractor thing" going for him. If you don't know what I'm talking about, spend a hot summer day watching a strapping young man haul hay, and you will have definitely found the up-side to being out in the country. Or, just watch a Kenney Chesney video. Brandon developed an immediate crush on me. This was too easy; I didn't even have to chase this one! I'm sure the reason for his infatuation was that I hailed from California, which was mysterious to him, since he had never been out of the state.

I may have told him I was just about to turn eighteen, but he found out that I was just sixteen once it was already too late. I had only added one year to my age, but statutory rape laws were the same in any state and a bit of a worry if my parents found out. However, it was all definitely consensual. So, I lied again, telling my mom he was seventeen and had lived near a nuclear power plant, which had caused a major growth spurt and an excess of facial hair when he was only twelve. "Just tragic," she said. We had the perfect summer romance. Brandon and I spent days at the lake and nights laying in the bed of his truck under the stars. I still wasn't ready to lose my virginity to a redneck, though. I could never bring him home to California. I mean, he had never even been to a Starbucks!

I went back to school, determined to find someone to teach all my new moves to. The beginning of that school year was unsuccessful. I went to Homecoming with a guy named Mike, who hung out with all the Asian break dancers (Mike was not Asian at all. He was a skinny white boy from Newport Beach). I tried to force my feelings for Mike, but I could not stop thinking about Brandon. I was afraid that I now knew what my mother had cursed my father for. I was experiencing my first taste of real love. When Mike asked me to start calling him "Milk," I decided that was the perfect time to end things.

Brandon and I would talk on the phone for hours every night. I had even convinced my parents to let me visit some friends in Tennessee over Christmas break, which I would obviously be using as a ruse to see Brandon, as well. I had all my friends at school jealous with tales of my romantic, southern college boyfriend. By Thanksgiving, I had decided I was ready to lose my virginity, and it was going to happen when I went back to the South to see Brandon, uh... I meant, my friends. I did enough research to complete a thesis on losing one's virginity. I always like to be prepared, so I had even gone to a local clinic to stock up on birth control pills and condoms. It wasn't until after sitting in the waiting room for hours amongst several other teenage girls that I realized this was an abortion clinic! Once I had found a sweet Spanish girl to translate to the "no comprende" nurse that I did not need a dirty hanger stuck into my vagina, I was sent on my way with a brown paper bag of generic brand condoms and, what I hoped was, legal birth control pills. I was ready and armed with enough latex to wrap a guy in condoms if needed!

I was staying with my friend, Vicky, and her mother for the week. Vicky's mom was hardly what you would call "strict". In fact, she hardly even gave a shit. She never asked what we were doing or where we were going. She would give us a curfew of 3:00 a.m., only because she didn't want to look bad to the other parents by not setting a curfew at all. I would be sitting outside on the front steps at midnight, with no fucking clue what there was to do in the middle of the night in such a small town, except ride around in a pickup truck or cook meth. Neither of which I was into. The only thing on my mind was pulling my V-card from the deck. I had told Brandon several weeks earlier that I wanted him to be the one. I was hoping this would give him enough time to plan the most romantic first time in history. Brandon claimed he had slept with three girls before. Cosmopolitan magazine told me that broke down to one.

> **Women usually reduce their number of sexual partners by three and men increase it by three. We always have to compensate for the opposite sex!**

Fine by me. I wanted someone with experience, not a venereal disease.

I was fantasizing about a romantic dinner followed by candles and an N'Sync ballad playing softly in the background. We had even planned to exchange Christmas presents that night, too. I just got him a card because I assumed that having sex with me was gift enough for him. He got me a gold bangle bracelet that I sold on Ebay several months later. I decided that it would be smarter to meet Brandon at his apartment instead of having him pick me up so Vicky's mom wouldn't be waiting for him to bring me home. Even though I doubt she would have ever been able to tell what time it was, given the wine-and-Paxil-induced coma she kept herself in. We told her that Vicky and I were staying at Katrina's house. Katrina was the only one with a car at the time so she drove us. Brandon had already found out I lied about my age, but he was cool with it since, as he said, I was "so mature for my age," and I agreed to let him keep lying to his friends about it. Katrina picked Vicky and me up, and we were off. They agreed to drop me off at Brandon's and then come back and get me later or the next morning.

Once we got to his apartment, we noticed that Brandon's overweight, thirty year-old roommate was there. Apparently, he was a friend of Brandon's family and was way behind in progressing as a normal adult. However, that still doesn't explain why he wanted to live in a small apartment with a nineteen year-old. I had thought this was supposed be a romantic night alone! Before I could find out when fatty was leaving, or hint around that he was not wanted, he was speeding off with Vicky and Katrina to buy them beer. I didn't want my friends to be sexually assaulted by a strange, overweight, and slightly balding man, but I was kind of hoping they wouldn't come back. I didn't have such luck. Brandon had just set out the romantic dinner he tried to cook for me when they returned with beer and pot. I tried to convince Katrina and Vicky to leave, but, as much of a creeper as Brandon's roommate was, he could buy them beer and roll a joint. They satisfied their munchies with my dinner and posted up in the living room like they were settling in for hibernation.

I was not going to let them ruin my first time. It had to be tonight because I was going home tomorrow and had already been lying to my friends at school about not being a virgin. My New Year's resolution was going to be to stop lying, so I decided the best way to do that was to make all of my previous lies come true. I couldn't talk my dad into buying me a Corvette, get a summer home in Hawaii, or make the lead singer of The Offspring my cousin, but I could damn sure lose my virginity!

Brandon and I went into his room to be alone. I was not thrilled that there were three other people on the other side of a wall that was as thin as the paper Snoop Dogg rolls his joints with. But beggars can't be choosers. We made out and did some heavy groping for what seemed like hours. I had started to get bored. Finally the clothes came off and the questions started. Yes, I felt like I was being interrogated: "Are you sure? Are you really sure? What kind of condom do you want me to use? Do you need a glass of water? Are you sure you're sure?" I couldn't fault the guy for covering his bases. What we were doing was illegal in most states, and I wouldn't have been surprised if he had asked me to sign a consent form or drive to South Dakota where it was legal to have sex with a minor.

I braced myself for what my sister and her friends told me was going to be a painful experience. I even popped an ibuprofen beforehand. Well, it really was not that bad.

Breaking the hymen sounds much more painful than it really is. I think the horror stories you hear are meant to be a tactic only to scare you into not doing it.

> **Adults will say anything to get kids to not have sex. I plan on telling my children that intercourse can cause deadly seizures.**

For me, sex for the first time didn't quite live up to the hype. I was expecting the multiple orgasms I had been reading about. I think Katrina, Vicky, and the creeper roommate got more excitement trying to listen to us from the other side of the door. A few thrusts and it was over. Where was my educational experience? I was counting on learning all I needed to know to return home a teenage, sexual prowess.

At the very least, I got the job done and accomplished what I set out to do. I was no longer a virgin, and I had four witnesses to back me up.

"Did I Really Do My Hair For *This*?"

So, I had been eyeing this hot mechanic for several weeks. He wasn't just hot; he was grease-on-your-hands, "check my oil, please" hot! I first saw him when I took my car in for a routine oil change and tire rotation. A few weeks later, my check engine light came on. YES! I went to the repair shop, and Mr. Mechanic was at the desk. I told him I needed someone to check under my hood, and he obliged. He said he would call when my car was ready and told me his name.

Could it be true? Could this be the answer to my only fear about getting married? I am neurotically attached to my last name. Since a best friend and I share the same first name, I have always been called by my last. I have often wondered: What will people call me if I ever get married and change my name? Will I even know what to answer to? Well, this grease monkey man had the same last name as I mine! I was now convinced it was destiny that had brought us together. I imagined how cute the wedding invitations would be, and I wondered if you could hyphenate your last name if both of them were the same.

So, I conducted my usual reconnaissance: Facebook stalking. I found my surname soul-mate and saw he was "single". So, I "friend requested" him and held my breath. I didn't just leave it there. I went a step further and sent him a message making sure it wasn't weird that I had stalked him on Facebook and friended him.

> I didn't think at the time that a message apologizing for being a stalker was a bit unorthodox. When he instant messaged me later that night saying it was not weird, I should have noticed that red flag: "No, sure I didn't mind. I love creepy girls with extremely good internet search skills."

Nope, I continued on in blind and oblivious bliss. I was ecstatic when he called and we spoke for almost two hours on the phone that night. I thought to myself: This is the first guy I have really liked in a long time. The last twelve, I didn't really know what I was doing. I thought I liked them, but, when they turned out to be douches, it had obviously been temporary insanity on my part for ever being attracted to them in the first place.

Mr. Mechanic called the next day and asked if I would like to hang out that night. Since it was a nice summer evening, he came by my house to have a few drinks on the porch. After a few Bud Light Limes and some just good enough conversation, I was ready to meet the family. Even though he dissed me with the one-armed hug, he still asked me out for the very next night when he left (Actions speak louder than words!). I woke up the next morning smiling and bouncing around like Miley Cyrus on a stripper pole at the Video Music Awards. He even called that afternoon to confirm our plans for 7:00 p.m. I even blow-dried my hair straight (If you have seen my curly-like-a-rabbi hair, you will know this was no small task)!

It was ten minutes to the beginning of the rest of my life!

7:15 p.m. I am the most punctual person on the planet. His tardiness was irritating, but I can overlook a few small flaws, right?

8:00 p.m. No mechanic.

8:30. I text him, "guess you didn't want to hang out." Duh! If he wanted to hang out, he would have shown up.

9:30. He butt-dials me! 9:31. I call back, and the butt answers. I overhear a redneck talking about a lawnmower. I call three more times in the next thirty minutes, with no answer.

10:00 p.m. I receive a text that says he just left his friend's baseball game and would be back in thirty minutes, if I still wanted to hang out.

10:05 p.m. I call my roommate for advice. She says to tell him, "no, I'm already out."

10:10. I text, "sure, if you want to."

Still waiting for that response.

Moral of the story: Don't get excited too quickly. If you have been pining over someone for months, or you think it's love at first sight, it probably isn't.

> **Take your friend's advice. Never take your own. You will just rationalize with yourself until you think your erratic behavior resembles that of a strong and independent woman.**

Postscript: The next day I got a brand new car and no longer needed to go to that repair shop.

Part Two

More Walk, Please!

I'm not the kind of Thoroughbred you take to the race and tie to the damn fence post. Lemme go!!

There are two kinds of people: "talkers" and "walkers". Big ideas and big talk are great, but let's see some action, people! Songs have been written about this. Does "a little less talk and a lot more action" ring a bell? Ever hear the phrase "let your walkin' do the talkin?" Men always talk about what they want to do or be in a relationship. Okay, I'm waiting. Don't tell me you are going to call me later. Just fucking call! The key to this is motivation. Or as I tell myself when motivation is needed:

> ### Get off your ass!!

Trying to Cut Through the Bullshit

So, I get a Facebook message from a friend-of-a-friend saying "hi." I say "hi" back. He asks me how I'm doing. I tell him that I'm good and ask him how he is doing, and he tells me he is doing fine. This meaningless messaging goes on all day. Finally, I ask him what's up and what he wants from me.

His response is, of course, "What do u want?"

This is so frustrating! This is probably how Lindsay Lohan feels after being couriered from the bar to rehab to jail and back to the bar. When does the vicious cycle stop? What is a girl to do?

> Apparently, this guy wants something from me. Is it a date, a casual rendezvous—or, do I just give off the impression that I enjoy beating around the bush and bullshitting all day on the computer? I DON'T!

The Facebook messaging transitions to texting, with still no end in sight. What happened to the good, old-fashioned phone call? It used to be as easy as call and ask a girl out, and then go out. Now, there are thousands of different technological steps to go through before actually making human contact. You friend-request me, I post on your wall. You message me back, I IM you with my number. You text me, I e-mail you back. Sometimes, there is never even a phone call. You can arrange a date with someone you barely know without ever hearing his voice! I love my technology, but a little old-fashioned phone call isn't totally out-of-date yet.

> **Bottom line:** If you want to get to know me, call and ask me out using real, audible words. Pick me up and take me on a real face-to-face date with actual conversation. If you just want to sleep with me, just come out and ask, so I can tell you what a douche you are. If you want to answer every question with a question, then don't bother.

One Girl's Dud is Another Girl's Orgasm

I ran into a girlfriend one night at a bar, and she started telling me about this new guy she had been dating. It turns out that I had gone out with him a few times years ago, but things never went anywhere. Not much personality, so-so looks, not too ambitious—just your average, everyday, small-town guy. Don't get me wrong: he was nice at first, but there was no spark. Every time I tried to get within six inches of him, he got all uncomfortable and started acting like a jack-ass. I figured he was gay and moved on.

My friend and I had a similar experience with this guy. He chased us both in the beginning, and we didn't care. But, wouldn't you know it, that, as soon as we started to reciprocate the interest, this average Joe turned into a douche bag? He was rude, cynical, and belittling. Pretty much like the boy that sat behind you in third grade that pulled your hair and made fun of you because he really liked you. The one big difference between mine and my friend's short affairs with this guy is that she got some physical action. When I was seeing him, he acted like he was afraid of girls. I even questioned his sexuality at one point. No sex, no foreplay, not even a kiss! I knew I hadn't lost my touch. I knew he was not disgusted by me. So, he must be a complete douche lord. I was over it as quickly as I assumed he was. Well, my friend tells me, though it only happened once or twice and there was a lot of alcohol involved, this guy was the best she'd ever had!

What?! Did hell just freeze over? Does my turkey bacon have wings? This guy was apparently a sexual dynamo. Maybe this was the same kind of experience Nick Lachey had with Jessica Simpson? Poor Nick never got much out of Jess, but John

Mayer said she was "sexual napalm!" Could my friend be this sleeper cell's John Mayer? Bestowing the "Best in Bed" award is not a small deal. You have to be pretty fucking amazing and extremely flexible to even make it to my Top Five. At first, I was a bit jealous. I thought: What's wrong with me? Did I not give him enough beer when I tried to get him drunk? Maybe hard liquor was his thing.

After I got over myself, I realized this: Good for him! And, even better for her! I am still acquaintances with this guy, and I have sometimes wondered when he would hit behavioral puberty. He still acts like a childish bully to the girls he likes.

> **He may not be able to communicate effectively with a female, but apparently he just walks the walk. No words needed. What I couldn't uncover, my friend uncorked. Snaps to her and all of you ladies that have turned a man that seems to be a complete bore into a bedroom champion! I raise my glass of vodka tonic to you.**

One Hand or Two?

'm not much of a one-night stand kind of girl. I have only had a few, and I don't like to think of them as one-night stands. I like to view them as a romantic and spontaneous start to a long and healthy relationship! Now, whether or not that relationship lasts longer than a few hours, varies by the subject. But, it's always best to at least start with good intentions. Then you don't feel as bad when it turns into a Category Five Shit Storm like this story.

I was at a bar with my then-new roommate. She knew a lot of people and a lot of guys (I'll have more on her later. Read: "You Might Be a Hooker If")! I thought: Yes, a whole untapped resource of men and my own live-in phone-a-friend to meet them!

So, back to this bar: I spotted a hot red-head by the dart board and pointed him out to the roomie. Although not many women do, I happen to find red-headed guys hot. She (no surprise here) knew him! Once she introduced me, I realized he was not that attractive up close and that maybe I needed to lay off the grape bomb shots. But, this dude seemed really into me. What the hell—I had been trying to not be so shallow, anyway!

After a nice conversation and a few more grape bombs, I drove him home (Red Flag #1: Where was this dude's car?). Anyway, we got to his house, and he invited me into the hot tub (Red Flag #2: A single guy has a hot tub for one reason. Haven't you watched the Jersey Shore?). This ginger wasn't a great kisser. This surprised me because red-heads are usually fire in the sexual area (pun fully intended). After a little hot tub make-out session, I dry off and attempt to make my exit. He offers to give me a massage. My neck had been sore for a while, and things were not going well with my hot chiropractor, so I accepted the rub-down.

Half-way into what seemed like an innocent neck massage, he asked me which flavor of massage oil I preferred (Red Flag #3: Either he just graduated from LMT school, or I had uncovered some pre-mature freakiness, in which case, I would have to be well into a serious relationship, or at least very intoxicated, before I could let my sexual freak flag fly). I was almost at a loss for words. It was the best massage I'd ever had that I didn't have to pay for. Especially when I closed my eyes and pretended he was Matthew McConaughey.

Since I didn't want to be rude, and he had almost worked out the knot on the left side of my neck, I went with vanilla. I noticed the silk scarves tied on the headboard, but I assumed they were to wipe off the massage oil. After all, it would be rude to send me home greasy. But, when my mahogany-haired masseur asked if I was, and I quote, "more comfortable with one hand or two tied up to start?" I freaked the fuck out.

Red Alert! We've got a veteran kinkster!! I flipped over and ran quicker than Michael Phelps dives underwater, and I got out of there. It was nice of him to ask first, but bondage isn't really my thing. I don't care if the scarves were Hermes. I jumped off that bed and ran to my car so fast, that I definitely pulled something and had to actually pay for another massage the next day. My second massage in a 24-hour period wasn't as good as the first, but, at least, I didn't have to worry that I may get tied up and date-raped by the masseuse at Massage Envy.

The Windex Man

I met this hot, Georgia boy when I was nineteen. He was spending the winter with some friends in Tennessee while he took a semester off from school. Or, from his probation officer, I'm still not quite sure. I stalked him to the best of my abilities for weeks. I would pump my friends for information constantly. Why go to the source when you can exhaust your friends with questions and demands to get what you want? I would bribe them with cigarettes and free cocktails to ask him what he thought about me. My go-to line was always, "Don't let him know it came from me." Of course, saying that is like putting it down in writing and adding your signature. He totally knew it came from me. This backwards behavior was pretty much my modus operandi every time I had a new crush.

> **As I have gotten more mature, and more disappointed with my friends' lack of work ethic on my behalf, I have learned that if you want something done right, it's best to do it yourself.**

So, my new best bud and I did everything together. Or everything that my crush was going to be doing, anyway. We would sit at her boyfriend's house and watch them watch sports. I would pretend to give a shit when she cried about how her mean boyfriend never paid any attention to her. Her boyfriend happened to be a huge prick, and she was a boring bitch, so that's not an impossible one to figure out. But, I went with it just to get a crack at my hot, Southern stud. I became part of this little foursome that finally broke into my long awaited twosome.

It wasn't as romantic as I had hoped meeting the love of my life would be, but there are things worse than a first date at Hooters. There were a few more cheap bar and grill meals, with a plethora of "2 for 1" well drinks and beer specials. He was sweet, though. He didn't have heat in his car, so he would drive forty-five minutes to my house in below-freezing temperatures, wrapped in a blanket and dressed like an Eskimo. The poor guy even had to keep a roll of paper towels in his car to wipe the fog from the windshield. We both went to a Christmas party separately with our own friends one night. He knew I was going to be there, but we hadn't planned on going together. We hadn't planned on leaving together, either. I immediately ditched my crew of girls that I came with to follow the Boring Bitch around all night and be near my crush. When B.B. and her boyfriend snuck off to do what I can only assume was cocaine in the bathroom (the only thing they could agree on was the drugs they liked), we had our chance to disappear into one of the empty bedrooms.

Now, my OCD causes me to feel dirty sleeping on three-day-old sheets, so getting naked in a strange bed with someone I barely knew made me shudder a bit. But, hey, you can't always have your cake and eat it, too. I was just drunk enough to totally forget about the possible bed bugs and the plan of seduction I had for him. I stumbled around trying to do a sexy stripper dance in my new lingerie that I had bought in the hope it might come in handy. I was a bit more intoxicated than I thought because I tried to pop and lock it, but ended up falling on the bed. He was pretty drunk, too, so neither of us wasted any time. We pretty much just got down to it. No making out, no foreplay, no "Are you sure?" "Yeah, are you sure?"

bullshit to tease each other and prolong what we both thought we wanted.

Don't think I am cutting things out or trying to leave out the juicy details, because the sex went just like this: a few misses upon entry, a grunt, a thrust, then, silence. This guy came in less than sixty seconds! He went from my future husband and father of my delinquent children to "that guy" in less than a minute. I was pretty disappointed. I felt like a little girl running downstairs Christmas morning to find no presents, no tree, and mommy fucking Santa Claus. I quickly realized that this relationship was going nowhere fast and I had to get out. I quickly dressed and made some bullshit excuse about how I was on roofie patrol and needed to go make sure my friends hadn't gotten anything slipped into their drinks. I put my panties back on inside-out, stuffed my $80 lace bra into my purse, and peaced out. I three-way called two girlfriends on the way home and told them the whole story, which was, actually, a very short story.

> **The phrase I chose to describe the encounter still follows that guy around to this day: "He was a Windex man—two pumps and a squirt". There really isn't anything else to say after that.**

The Whiskey Dick

I have always been pretty lucky in the penis department. The majority of the ones I have dealt with have been average to larger-than-average in size. I believe that size doesn't matter, and it truly is about how you work the equipment to its maximum performance. But, even the most objective and fair girl has her limits. Unfortunately, I am not her. I have encountered huge, elephantiasis dicks that were in no way going near any hole in my body without a gallon of lube and a skilled surgeon in the room. I have also encountered a few that were quite possibly so small, they could have been compared to my Chihuahua Artie's penis. Artie is a small dog and neutered. So, what's your excuse?

I met this guy named Cameron at the beginning of one of the first summers after I moved to Tennessee. He was from Atlanta, and his parents had a huge summer farm just outside of Nashville. He would come up on the weekends, and we began spending a lot of time together. Cameron was a pretty cool guy. He was cute, smart, and twenty-one. Since I was nineteen, it scored huge points that he could buy my friends and me alcohol. He sure wasn't into buying girls flowers or gifts; his idea of a gift was a box full of purple "hooter shooters" that come in those test tube shots and a carton of cigarettes (I do love being spoiled!). We would talk during the week while he was back at home, working to inherit his family's fortune. I had no idea what his family did, but I did know that Cameron went out to lunch a lot and played golf with his dad's business partners. I would day-dream that I would soon be moving to Atlanta with him, and live in his huge home, and drink sweat tea, and have a maid that I called "Aunt Jemima".

Every Friday afternoon, I was giddy waiting for him to get into town. One particular weekend we attended a field party. It's pretty much your regular party, except it's outside with a bunch of trucks and most of the alcohol is homemade.

I still don't understand how a California girl like me ended up in the South and actually loves it here! So, if it means that you think I am a bit country, then, that's fine. But, the most expensive liquors in the world can't get you drunk like homemade wine or moonshine. It's a buzz that feels almost like mixing alcohol and ecstasy without the chance of ending up in the ER, hopefully!

After two solo cups of this homemade wine, I was horny and ready to leave with Cameron. We went back to his family's house that was empty for the weekend. Some hardcore making out and hours of the normal fooling around eventually led to what was about to be our first time having sex. I had never thought about what he was packing in his pants. All the dicks I had come in contact with in my life so far were not disappointing. I pretty much thought penis size was in direct correlation to body proportion. He wasn't a midget, so I never assumed there would be anything to worry about.

We began to take each other's clothes off, and, when I reached in his boxers, I couldn't find anything. It was like digging around in the bottom of your purse for your mini mascara. I finally found it (or, the lack thereof), and it was small and soft. The fact that it was so small was disappointing, but I could have rolled with that. However, this was my first encounter with a flaccid penis, and it was something I will never forget. I jerked my hand out of there like it had tried to bite me! Not that it would have even been able to though.

Basically, I'm a picky eater because I have issues with texture. I do not like anything mushy.

Same goes for male body parts. Who doesn't like a hard ass, hard abs, and a hard penis? Cameron tried to act like it wasn't a big deal. I hoped this didn't happen to him on a regular basis. He even asked me to jerk him off! I'm sorry, but giving hand-jobs is something I retired in tenth grade and doing it now makes me feel like one of those girls pumping the batter at Hot Dog on a Stick. I don't even like a guy trying to finger me.

> **Don't try to do something I can do better! That's why you have your mouth. Use it for something that I can't do to myself.**

The look on my face must have given Cameron the hint pretty quickly, because he then proceeded to jerk himself off. "NOOOO!" I screamed. "Don't do that!" He replied, "Oh, do you want to suck me off instead?" I wanted to say, "No, you dumb fuck! I don't want to go anywhere near that thing until you put it in water and it hardens and expands to its normal size! Like some kind of dick chia pet!" What I actually said was, "Uh, is there anything we can do to fix it?" I'm all about teamwork, so long as I don't have to touch it or watch him jack off like a primate on meth. "Shit, I'm sorry. I must have a case of the whiskey dick," he said. "But, you have been drinking beer all night," I rebutted. "No", he said, "you don't understand. Sometimes alcohol makes it hard for a guy to get going, y'know?"

This didn't make a lot of sense to me, since, the drunker I get the more I want to have sex. Men and women really are different. I first learned the basic differences in a school janitors' closet with Daniel Hankins in first grade, and this was yet another lesson.

I really liked Cameron, so I decided that I would forget about this and give him another chance. I'm not so shallow that a small penis and too much beer would make me not like him anymore. The next night we went to dinner. He got kind of pissed when I asked him not to drink. I just explained that I wanted it to be "bigger" tonight. Whoops. Guess the whiskey dick doesn't affect size, too. He got up to go to the bathroom. I figured he needed a minute to cool off, and I definitely needed some time to figure out what I was going to say to get myself out of this one. Twenty minutes and three Jack-and-Cokes later, I realized he had left. Well, I had actually realized it after the first drink, but the waiter was pretty hot. I paid the check, left my number for the cute waiter, and went home.

I tried to call Cameron several times to try and apologize, but he would not answer or return my calls. I continued to call the rest of the weekend, to no avail. I even called his house in Atlanta hoping to reach him. I was surprised when a girl answered the phone. She rudely asked who I was, and then she told me she was Cameron's live-in girlfriend. I tried to apologize, but she kept grilling me about how I knew Cameron and asking what I wanted.

I simply explained to her that he left dinner the night before looking very ill, and I was just calling to check and see if his case of the whiskey dick was any better.

Project Safari

Let me start by saying that I am not a racist. I don't know why, but black guys love me. Ninety-percent of my Match.com inbox is black guys. When I walk by, they stare and always make comments about my ass. I don't have a Kardashian ass, or anything impressive like that, although I do suppose it is a bit "bootylicious." This got me thinking that maybe I should get to know my new fans a bit better. I wanted to see what this was all about. All I had ever heard is that they have huge hardware and are great in bed, but I wanted to know if the black guys in the South were more sexy-and-smooth, like Usher, or nasty, like Flava Flav.

I had no intention of having a one-night-stand, or even looking for a black guy to date; I just wanted to indulge my curiosity. So, I put on my most ass-hugging dress and some extra bronzer, and I went for it! If I didn't land a Chocolate Casanova tonight, I could at least catch the attention of any random white guy wearing Ed Hardy. Remember, at this time I was living in a college town in the South. There weren't really any black people at the bars I went to, unless they were gay or worked there. And I didn't think going to Club 187 next to the freeway to find them was a safe idea for my first time.

So, I stuck to the most diverse bar I could find without a metal detector at the door. It didn't take me long to spot a subject of choice. He was tall, built, with blue eyes, and was a very creamy-like shade of what I'd like to think of as "Non-Fat Mocha." All I had to do was the "two-second look," and he was heading over to my table.

> **A male friend of mine taught me the Two-Second Look, and he claimed it had a 99% success rate. You just look down, lock eyes with your intended target, giving him that "take me now" stare for a count of two, then coyly look down and away. I found a much lower success rate until I got Lasik and overcame my blinking problem caused by severe eye dryness.**

Anyway, his fine ass swaggered over, and he told me his name was Darrin. I was a bit disappointed, since I was hoping for a "LaDamien," "DeShawn," or a "Tyrell," but beggars can't be choosers. Darrin told me that his dad was African-American and his mom was French. So, he was pretty much half-black and half-white (He probably just thought that saying "French" instead of "white" sounded sexier. And, after a few cranberry vodkas, it did sound sexier to me).

Okay, so he wasn't the dark-chocolate-deep-in-the-jungle-R-Kelly-combination I had intended, but he did play college football and that scored extra points with me. Being a college athlete means several things to me: you are hot by association, you have a good body, and you have lots of sex; which makes you experienced in bed. And, most importantly, there is a small chance that I could fulfill my fantasy of dating a professional athlete—until, of course, he gets injured or accused of rape. Darrin continued to talk about his college football days and his love of R&B music. Well, shit, he wasn't going pro, but, hey, I was just doing research, anyway.

After I had switched to drinking gin-and-juices, because I wanted to fully immerse myself in the culture, Darrin got extra friendly. He was rubbing on the small of my back and kissing on my neck. This actually made me a bit uncomfortable. I am not really the PDA type. I don't mind a hug here, some hand-holding there, maybe even a peck on the mouth. But, when someone I just met an hour ago tries to nuzzle me to death in a bar, it is not okay. The only thing that was okay, or rather hilarious actually, was the reaction of my friends.

I'm pretty sure my girlfriends thought I had been roofied. They were all from the South, born and raised. These girls weren't members of the Ku Klux Klan or anything, but they definitely weren't down with the darkness. Growing up in Southern California, I was raised to be pretty open-minded and able to adapt to different situations. It also comes in as a handy excuse, because I can pretty much do or say anything I want and blame it on being from L.A. and parented by hippies or cholos or Jewish Hollywood agents, all of which my parents were none.

Darrin began asking me to go to his house with him.

> **I prefer not to go to a guy's house. It's so much easier to kick a creeper out of your own home than escaping from his. If threatening to call the cops doesn't work, asking him what he wants for breakfast and inviting him to church with you the next morning always does. It also saves you from ever having to do a walk of shame. Make one down the halls of a frat house the morning after a toga or "Wild Eighties" party, and you'll see my point.**

My friend Caroline was riding home with me, so I figured she would at least try to save me from this experiment gone wrong. Thank goodness for her! She took one look at Darrin and flipped. Caroline is from Mississippi. She had worked really hard at suppressing her trashy, redneck tendencies, but black people, whiskey, and NASCAR tended to trigger them.

She physically pulled me away from the conversation I was having with him about how I didn't feel comfortable going to the projects at night. He assured me that he did not live in the projects or the ghetto, but Caroline had already dragged me half-way out of the bar (I only pretended to protest her a bit so I wouldn't seem like a total bitch)! Caroline said she couldn't let me go home with him because he had that "rapist look". I wasn't really sure what the "rapist look" was, but I assumed it meant you wore dark hoodies and drove a white, windowless van.

I went to bed that night disappointed, yet still curious about my cocoa mystery man. Darrin called a few days later to ask me out. Fortunately, I was on my way out of town and asked for a rain check when I was back after Thanksgiving break. Hallelujah! Another thing to be thankful for: easy excuses! I was still a bit curious about him, though, so I Googled Darrin and found his Facebook page.

All of his female friends were white, and he had tons of pictures of himself mounted on cute, little brunette girls that looked strikingly similar to me! Did Darrin have some kind of fetish for JAPs? By that, I mean "Jewish American Princesses," not the Asian ones. My whole platform for this fact-finding mission had been shattered. The tables had been turned. The player may have very well been played. However, I did have more reason to give thanks: I hadn't become another notch on Darrin's big, black belt. I doubt I will ever venture out into the jungle again.

Part Three

College by the Numbers

Two for the Price of One

Every Thursday night in college, as my best friend Katrina and I would be driving to happy hour at Chili's, we would see these two really cute twins taking their evening jog near the fraternity houses. They were really cute in that cross-country, short-water-polo-player kind of way. Their bouncing blond curls would flop in unison as they ran along the road. We would see them two or three times a week running. Yes, we did enjoy Chili's "2 for 1 Margaritas" on a regular basis.

It took a few years of not going out until 10:00 p.m. and dragging my hung-over ass to an 8:00 a.m. class (or not showing up at all), but I finally figured out that happy hour was better for both my check book and my grades.

> **I could get drunker for cheaper and still be home in bed by midnight to get to my class in the morning. Colleges should give those kinds of tips out at freshman orientation.**

Anyway, we spotted the twins again at our regular Wednesday night bar. We had a regular place for every night of the week, in case we chose to pull an all-nighter. All-night partying, that is, not studying. This place was a country/college bar. There was line dancing until 10:00 p.m., then the booty-shaking rap music would come on and the co-eds would grind on the dance floor. Once a month, the bar even did a Wet T-Shirt/Mechanical Bull-Riding Contest. You couldn't find a classier place, unless you were on spring break in the Florida panhandle.

We tried to decide which twin we each wanted, but the little bastards were identical. I went for the shorter one, since I was shorter than Katrina. Their heights were literally the only ways you could tell them apart! I approached Tweedle Dee, and Katrina followed my lead with Tweedle Dum. They talked like hippies, saying "for sure" and "right on" every chance they got. They also had an odd obsession with Guns 'N' Roses and both majored in Public Relations. However, they obviously had not passed Communication 101, because I could never tell if they were talking to one of us, each other, or just to themselves.

We still let them drive us home, even though they begged us to come to their apartment and listen to the Best of Axel Rose Live album. I was afraid they might have bunk beds, and, although I loved Katrina like a sister, I wasn't ready for that kind of foursome. We each made out with our respective twin that night, and they even asked us both out. We really were not sure if this was going to be two individual dates or a double date. I was relieved when it was a double date, because the two of these guys together could barely make up one suitable date.

But what the twins lacked in brains, they made up for in fun! Before long, the four of us were going out and partying every night. We would all share a booth at Waffle House at three in the morning and told the other drunken, late-night customers that there was only one guy with us: "You must be drunker than we are if you're seeing double!" The only time I was alone with Tweedle Dee was when Katrina and Tweedle Dum would go upstairs to her room.

Mine turned out to be the shyer twin, and I felt like a horny, teenage boy when I would urge

Tweedle Dee to put his hands up my shirt. He warmed up and got more comfortable after a few weeks, and we finally did the deed. After that night, Tweedle Dee seemed a bit anxious all the time, which Tweedle Dum found hilarious. He was always making fun of his twin brother for being on edge all the time. Katrina finally told me that Tweedle Dum had told her that his brother had a girlfriend. They were on a break, but sleeping with me made him think he might want her back.

Gee, nothing like being the girl that makes a guy realize how much he loves his ex. It didn't bother me that much because I was already growing bored with him; it wasn't like I was going to marry Tweedle Dee. Since he and the girlfriend were technically on a break, I didn't feel that I had done anything wrong, or that I was the scarlet-lettered "other woman". Because I simply wasn't. Or so I had thought.

I found out a few nights later that Tweedle Dee had not informed her of the break. As far as she was concerned, he was still her boyfriend. Wow, a busy guy like that sure did need a twin! I decided to confront him about it that night. He brought over schnapps, and I got distracted. Tweedle Dee and I began making out in my living room. Then, the door bell rang. I looked through the glass door and saw a small girl, about my age, with her arms crossed and tapping her foot. I'm no body language expert, but I could tell she was pissed. Before I could even wonder who it was, I heard what sounded like a dead body hitting the floor. Tweedle Dee had dropped to the fetal position in my living room and hid behind my couch! He said, "I'm really sorry, but do not open the door!" The fear in his eyes told me exactly who it was.

Maybe I should have been the one apologizing to him, since I did answer the door. She introduced herself as Tweedle Dee's girlfriend and demanded that he come outside to talk. He was still not-so-conspicuously hiding behind the couch when I told her I hadn't seen him, and I was sorry she was dating such a dumb-ass. She insisted that she knew he was in there, and she wasn't leaving until he came out. I shut the door and turned around to see him crawling on all fours to my bedroom. "Hey genius, it's a glass door, she can see you!" I yelled at him. He scurried into my bedroom and proceeded to tell me pretty much what I already knew.

The girlfriend finally left, and Tweedle Dee was so flustered that he went outside to smoke a cigarette. He never came back. I waited for about an hour, figuring he was on the phone with her or something. Then, I imagined, he would come back in, groveling for my forgiveness, and I would tell him how much of a douche he was and show him the door. But, that didn't happen. I was pissed. How dare he not return to receive the cussing he deserved! I tried to call him many times, with no success. I didn't hear from him for days. I had finally let it go and decided that he was too cowardly for me, anyway.

The next weekend, I was rolling a joint in Katrina's living room with her roommate, and suddenly, Tweedle Dum walked in. After some shameless compliments I doled out about his hair and fresh tan, he told me what happened to his brother that night after he left my house. Tweedle Dee had actually jogged three miles from my house to his girlfriend's house that night to beg for her forgiveness! Un-fucking believable. He could have at least called a cab or leisurely walked. **Running made it sound like he was running away from me!** A soul-searching moonlight stroll would have been better than a sprint back to his girlfriend's!

However, I got my revenge each time I heartlessly rejected him whenever he would "booty call" me at four in the morning. Katrina and Tweedle Dum weren't meant for the long-haul, either. One night, after drinking too much at a party, he pissed in her cat's litter box. She chased him out of her house wielding a bottle of Lysol like it was mace. I decided that if Katrina and I wanted to spend more time together, we should just stick to Chili's happy hour instead of dating twins ever again.

Puppy Love

Why do guys think that giving a puppy to a girl is a good idea? One summer, it seemed like all of my friends were getting cute, furry, cuddly puppies wrapped in bows from their boyfriends. We were in college; why would you want any kind of responsibility? It was hard enough cleaning up after yourself and geting to class on time—who needs a piddling puppy to clean up after, too! "Here ya go, baby, I got you a puppy, so you can clean up its shit, feed it, walk it, and pay for all the shots, food, and toys it will need." Guys think they are so smart. The money you will have to spend on that dog will probably cost you three times as much than what they paid the guy at the puppy mill! Oh, but, wait: "He's soooo adorable and has a cute bow and puppy breath! Awwww!"

I will admit it, I was jealous. I wanted my boyfriend to gift me a puppy as a public profession of his love, too. And, I love puppy breath! But, my boyfriend Adam was a cheap fuck. His idea of a nice dinner was the free peanuts at Logan's and splitting the "2 for 1" beer. The nicest gift he ever got me was a knock-off Chanel purse that said "Channel" on the inside of the "Made in China" tag. It seemed like suddenly all of my girlfriends were going to the dog park together to show off the proof that they had good boyfriends. Dammit, I wanted one, too! Or rather both: the puppy and a good boyfriend.

However, I had not had much luck with pets in the past. There was the kitten that I was convinced was possessed by the devil. I would walk into my apartment to find claw marks on the walls and this mangy feline swinging from the curtains. I gave her away to a friend that said he would "take care of her", but I have my suspicions that the evil, little bitch never made it past the freeway overpass. Then, there was the cute puppy I paid way too much for at the pet store. I named him Dave because the boy I liked at the time was a big Dave Matthews Band fan. I did not like DMB's music, and Dave the Dog shit on my brand new Laura Ashley comforter. He now has a good home with another family. At least, that is what the bum I gave him to promised. It was understandable that anyone would question my ability to care for a pet in the long-term. But, I figured that, since I was now in a serious relationship, it would be much easier to raise a dog in a two-parent home.

Adam wasn't having it. He wasn't going to spend good money on something he had to help take care of. Of course, he wasn't spending money on anything. I realized there was no way he would loosen the grip on his wallet and get me anything more than a stuffed dog from Build-A-Bear. Remember: "If you want something done right, you just have to do it yourself."

Chihuahuas were the most popular dog at the time, thanks to Paris Hilton, and I was all for buying more designer purses to carry it around in. I searched the paper for a Chihuahua breeder (I had learned my lesson after the last demon dog I got at the pet store took a shit on my comforter). I needed to see what kind of home environment this puppy was coming from. But Adam wouldn't even go with me to pick him out! He would be paying for it later, though—literally. I pulled up to the breeder's house expecting to see puppies frolicking through the grass, playing with Charmin toilet paper, and rolling in the dandelions.

I reached the end of a long and desolate gravel driveway to find a mobile home with an old school bus parked in back. An overweight woman with barely any teeth and a walking cane answered the door. She took me around back to the kennel. I quickly realized, due to her two lazy eyes and how she was banging around on shit with her cane, that this woman that advertised herself as a "world champion dog breeder" was fucking blind! I still had not learned my lesson with Craigslist: "You should always ask for references first." The "kennel" was the gutted out school bus. There were at least thirty yapping Chihuahuas in that thing! I really wished Adam had been there, then. I just wanted to see the look on his face when the breeder started pointing out the prettiest ones! How did she know what the prettiest ones were? She was fucking blind!

As she was pointing out pieces of dog shit instead of actual puppies, I spotted one little feisty Chihuahua trying to hump two other ones at the same time. He was only a few weeks old and already trying to talk bitches into a threesome! That was my dog! He was the perfect shade of blonde, and any puppy that was confident enough to take on two females at once could definitely hang with me. I scooped up my new friend and was proud of myself for rescuing him from such a horrible life with the blind, crazy lady. I was like Daddy Warbucks taking Orphan Annie (with a tail) to her new home! Except, I made sure my new puppy was a male because I felt that there should always be a constant male figure in my life.

I cleaned him up and put a big red bow on him and took him over to Adam's. He thought the puppy was really cute, until I stuffed the dog in a box, tied it with a bow and told Adam to practice presenting me with "his gift" while I set up the camera. I had it perfectly staged and even captured my best surprised face to show to my friends. After a few takes and some adjustments to the lighting, I quizzed Adam on the details so our stories were straight, such as how he had decided that I was such an amazing girlfriend and that this would be the first step toward our own little family. I made sure he knew all the specifics about the blind, toothless breeder and the school bus kennel to corroborate the story with our friends. I knew he thought I was crazy, but he went along with it because, for the first time, he felt guilty for being such a cheap-ass. Maybe even a little jealous that the puppy was keeping me more entertained than he was.

When I told my dad, he asked me if I was on drugs or running my own puppy mill. He said, "Any girl that buys herself a dog and lies to everyone so they will think she has a great boyfriend is bat shit crazy." In fact, he was surprised I even had a boyfriend at all. With such parental encouragement, I decided that I would name the puppy after my dad, just to spite him. It would also give me a good excuse when I got mad and cussed my dad. I could just say the dog shit on the floor. That is how Artie came into my life. He was so much cuter than the puppies my friends had. None of their dogs had Coach carrying bags and their own wardrobes, which I had also guilted Adam into pretending he had bought for me, too. Yes, I was that girl. That is, until Paris Hilton started collecting monkeys, then I stopped making Artie wear clothes.

When a month had gone by and I hadn't tired of the dog yet, I knew we were in for the "committed relationship" long-haul. I usually grow bored with things after three weeks. Unfortunately, I had grown bored with Adam. I tried to salvage our relationship by spicing up our sex life. The poor guy already felt like a bitch, so he was definitely not cool with me wanting to tie him up. So, I found someone else with a tongue ring that was cool with it. However, I had forgotten that Adam and I had planned to take Artie to the dog park the next morning, and he caught me red-handed. I tried to explain to him that we were just working on a "sleep study" together for my Human Behavior class, but those kind of excuses had stopped working when I changed my major from Psychology to Fashion Merchandising.

I tried to negotiate visitation rights with Adam for Artie, but, ultimately, I decided one unstable parent was better than two nut-jobs. I was grateful to Adam, though, because, if it had not been for him, I never would have gotten Artie. There may have been another boyfriend that would have really gotten me a puppy, but it wouldn't have been the same. Because Adam was so cheap and never thought to do anything considerate for me, I got the perfect dog myself and in my own way. He is still, to this day, the best and longest relationship I have ever had. The dog I mean, of course. Not the boyfriend.

Friends and Faces

Katrina had been hooking up with this really hot frat boy for a few months in college. She and I had begun hanging out with a few of his frat brothers, and we were all becoming close friends. These guys had weird nicknames given to them by the older guys in the fraternity. Like, the guy that always talked about where he was from, they called "Hometown". The guy that never kept his room clean was called "Dusty". The white kid from South Africa was dubbed "El Negro" (I never really understood that one). Katrina's Flavor of the Month had been given the name "Face" because all the girls loved his pretty, baby face. However, I believed it was probably because he always gave 110% effort in performing oral sex.

After Katrina tired of Face, she gave me the green light to pursue. Katrina had great taste in guys, and she never had a problem with me taking them for a second spin around the block. We did not view it as "sloppy seconds." More like "imitation is the best form of flattery." For Christ's sake, two of my serious relationships were with guys she had gone on dates with first, and then set them up with me. I like to think of it as my best friend pre-screening guys for me.

Face was not very hard to land. A short skirt and some average beer got his attention every time. He was the typical frat boy that just wanted to fuck as much as possible. But, I quickly learned why it didn't work out with Katrina. Face wasn't that great in bed. Granted, he was only nineteen, but pounding as fast as one can isn't fun for the one getting pounded. Our semi-romantic relationship ended quickly, but we became great friends. He was like the hot, big brother I never had. He introduced me to all of his fraternity brothers, which provided me with years of entertainment throughout college.

Face was a bit of a kleptomaniac, though. He would steal steaks from the grocery store to grill for dinner and take ties from department stores even though he never wore a tie. He actually stole things everywhere we went. Not because he couldn't afford to buy them, but, because, he claimed, George Bush was stealing from him, and it was only fair. Besides his fetish for theft, he was one of the best friends I had in college. I even brought Face home to California for Thanksgiving one year. I made it very clear to my parents that he was not my boyfriend. Of course they did not believe me, until they saw him making out with the neighbor. My sister, Beth, thought he was gay and asked him if he preferred to be the masculine one in his relationships, even though he seemed more like the flaming kind. He had to convince her he wasn't by making out with the neighbor....again.

One summer, Face introduced me to his fraternity brother named Sam and his girlfriend, Erica. Sam's reputation of being a hard-partier preceded him. Therefore, he didn't even need a nickname to make him seem cool. Face, Sam, Erica, and I were lying around the pool at the apartment complex we all lived at. The sweltering heat and humidity were miserable and even a dip in the pool wasn't easing my hot flashes. We all agreed that this would be much more enjoyable near the ocean, and we wished we were at the beach.

The bullshitting quickly turned into action, and we all packed up and drove down to the beach that night. That's what I loved about hanging out with Face and his friends. You never knew what could happen or what county jail you may end up in. Face was dating a girl named Cassidy at the time. Cassidy wasn't much fun, so she didn't get invited. He didn't even bother to call her and mention he was leaving town. None of us gave his lack of decency a second thought. We drove all night to Panama City Beach and found the cheapest motel room that didn't look like someone had been raped or murdered in it.

The next day, the four of us lay on the beach, drank beer, and played the occasional game of "Bury Sam in the Sand" while he was passed out. That night, we decided to have our own bonfire. Face was kind enough to steal all the supplies for us. I had no idea where he put it all, but the beer was cold and the steaks didn't seem contaminated, so I was cool. However, after not hearing from her boyfriend for twelve hours, Cassidy began calling over and over again. Fearing that she would come looking for him, Face told her he had been in the library studying and was probably going to be pulling another all-nighter. It was July. Maybe she thought he was in summer school. Still, this kid didn't even know where the library was. It's unbelievable how stupid some girls can be!

After that situation was handled and a few more bowls were smoked, we all had the munchies for pizza. We went to a local pizza place on the beach. Sam, Erica, and I were enjoying our meal when we heard glass breaking. We must have been so high that we never noticed that Face had left the table. He had just gone into the restroom, for reasons no one will ever know, and his drunk-ass decided to break the bathroom mirror! With his head! Face didn't like to smoke pot, so what he lacked in drug use, he made up for in alcohol intake. Only someone ridiculously inebriated would decide to crack a mirror with his head.

The owner of the pizza place started screaming and banging on the bathroom door. He finally got the door open, but Face had escaped out of the window! When the owner started questioning us about our friend, I decided to lie and tell him he was just some homeless kid we offered to feed on our way here, after our church group had let out. I also noted that I was pretty sure he was mentally retarded (That way, when the police came, he might have the option to plead insanity). Then, all of a sudden, the bathroom door burst open, and Face lunged around the restaurant owner and darted out the back. We decided it'd be best if the rest of us made our exit then, too. As we left, the owner phoned the cops. We figured it was probably time to end our little beach trip and get out of town before we had to waste our money on bailing Face out of jail or paying his hospital bill.

But, first, we had to find the dumb-ass. He wasn't anywhere nearby, so we decided to go back to the motel and wait. When we arrived back at the motel, there was a huge party going on. Tons of college kids were going from room to room, taking shots and funneling beers. Since there was no use in waiting alone, we joined the party. Sam told some random guy about our missing friend, and the random guy said he was just there and had done a funnel. We figured he couldn't have gotten far, so we looked next door. Same story: "Yeah, that dude was just here, he funneled a beer and left".

This trend repeated for several room parties, when we finally spotted him walking down the stairs to the beach. Well, not really walking. Two rather large girls were helping him to the beach. He had his shirt tied around his bloody head, from putting it through the mirror at the pizza place, and each arm around the two Shamus' necks. We finally talked him out of what he said was going to be an "awesome threesome on the beach with two really hot chicks".

As we sped out of town, there were two cop cars at the pizza place taking what I'm sure was Face's description. When we asked him why he'd punched a bathroom mirror, he answered, "Because I forgot to get extra parmesan for my pizza". About thirty miles from home, the mirror-punching kleptomaniac threw a drunk fit because he wanted McDonald's. I was so fed up with his shit and so pissed that we had to leave the beach that I just gave in. I was too tired, and maybe still even a bit too drunk to argue. I found the nearest McDonald's and let him have at it. He fell out of the car mumbling something about extra cheese, pickles, and special sauce. Then, I changed my mind. I'm never too anything to put up a fight!

I decided it was time to teach Face a lesson. I threw the car in drive, and, as I sped out of the McDonald's parking lot, I screamed out the window that he could shove his quarter-pounder up his ass. If he had managed to avoid jail in Florida, I figured he would be resourceful enough to find his way thirty miles home. But, when the three of us got back to our apartment complex, the bastard was already there! He was jumping around waving his arms in the air like he had just won the Daytona 500. He claimed he had caught a ride on the back of what he thought was a woman's motorcycle.

Fortunately, Face couldn't celebrate his victory for too long before his girlfriend, Cassidy, showed up. She freaked out when she saw his still-bloodied scalp. His explanation: a heated debate over the Dewey Decimal system at the library.

> **Only one of my friends could have come up with such a ridiculous alibi. They must be taking tips from me.**

That's How I Roll

After the Florida trip, Face was a bit heartbroken over Cassidy breaking up with him. I knew she would never believe his "trapped in the library" story. Face didn't even know where the library on campus was! He decided to lay low for a while, and I continued hanging out with his friends Sam, a guy from South Africa they called "El Negro", and another one of their hot fraternity brothers named Brad. I loved hanging with these guys because they were so much fun, but I had also developed a bit of a crush on Brad. I was down to do anything they suggested because they could turn the stupidest idea into an afternoon of crying-in-laughter fun. And, I got to be around my new crush. One day, they had wanted me to pull them on skis behind my car (even though it was the middle of May). Sure! Sounds fun! "Come on, Steph. Blow off your class and let's go throw beer bottles at road signs!" Sounds like a fabulous idea!

So, I didn't flinch when they asked me to go to the strip club with them. I had seen more of what was on that pole than these guys probably had, anyway. But, going to a strip club at noon with a lunch buffet? Only a man could come up with that kind of marketing plan. Men have a tendency to make mundane or even ridiculously stupid activities into something fun. Take sports for example. I love sports, but, when it comes down to it all, most of them really just consist of getting an object into a hole. Sound familiar?

I can't be the first person in the world that has related sports back to sex. Why do you think men have such a natural love for both? They are biologically designed to put anything they can into a hole! But, these male geniuses don't stop there. They add the spirit of competition and some trash-talking, and that's how you get every professional sports league featured on ESPN. For example, El Negro was obsessed with playing Frisbee Golf. Yes, it is exactly what you think it is: a simple combination of two boring sports that becomes Americas' new favorite pastime once alcohol and hot college guys are added to the equation.

Anyway, I had almost become like a little sister to these guys. This was great, except that I wanted to sleep with Brad. So, when on what seemed to be turning into a pretty boring weekend, Sam told me that he had gotten some ecstasy for all of us to do later that night, I thought, "Why the hell not?!"

My drug use had pretty much peaked at the occasional joint and eating 'shrooms on my annual trip to the local music festival. This actually happened to be one of the largest music festivals in the country and only thirty minutes from where I lived. I'm not a hippie, and camping in the mud without a shower for three days is not my idea of a good time. Conditions like that would normally send me into panic mode. But, I like the carefree hippie attitude and their homemade body oils, so I indulge myself once a year.

> *I can handle a three-day music festival in the mud and blistering heat as long as I have a steady supply of magic mushrooms and baby wipes.*

I had heard that ecstasy was a lot like 'shrooms. I knew that 'shrooms made me super friendly and made sex even better. If directed at the right subject, it could be just what I was looking for to have a fun night with Brad. We had already hooked up a few times, but, to be honest, he was a bit vanilla in bed. So, maybe a few sprinkles of ecstasy would loosen him up.

I should probably stop and say that, if you need to use drugs to get a guy to like you or sleep with you, then that is not a good sign. You should probably reevaluate your goals. The extreme version of this kind of behavior is why Lindsey Lohan became a lesbian. Even using alcohol is perfectly acceptable, as long as no roofies are involved. It's one thing to get someone drunk to loosen up. Guys have been getting girls drunk and in bed since the beginning of time. But, using ecstasy as a flirting tool could make for the plot of a Law and Order SVU episode. Don't worry about me, though, because, in true form, my master plan didn't go quite as planned.

The Three Fraternity Stooges and I prepared for our night of trippy over-indulgence. We stocked up on House music CDs, bought several cases of water, and a family size tub of Vick's Vapor Rub (I didn't know what the Vick's was for, but the guys assured me it would be awesome). We started out at the only dance club in our college town. The four of us found a nice, chill spot in what they called the "upstairs lounge". The upstairs lounge was really a renovated attic with old couches and low lighting and a girl manning the beer tub. I was excited to roll for the first time. "Rolling" is what it's called when you do ecstasy. I think they should rename it from "rolling" to "being thrown off a cliff to your death." But I hadn't discovered that yet.

At Sam's suggestion, I started with half of an ecstasy pill since it was my first time. Now, I think the guys were acting a bit more tripped out than they really were, because I wasn't feeling shit. Sam was swaying back and forth to what I think was India Arie. Brad was rubbing the leg of my jeans like he was petting the softest and furriest puppy he had ever come across. El Negro kept asking me over and over again if I heard that. "Do you hear that? It's so amazing, like the music is coming from inside my ears!"

All I could hear was the bad House music the DJ was playing and the sounds of three guys acting like total pussies. Although, as stupid as they were acting, they did seem to be having a hugely amazing time. I only felt full from all the water I had drunk to prevent dehydration. At the time, Sam had told me it was crucial to drink tons of water because ecstasy dehydrates you so much, you could die. I later learned from some hippies at a Widespread Panic concert that this really only applies to eating mushrooms. The only people that die from dehydration while on drugs are the stupid, or Kurt Cobain-type hardcore junkies, or otherwise people that happen to be rolling in the Sahara.

I wanted to get on everyone else's level, so I took the other half of my pill, and then another one for good measure. It took about thirty minutes before I felt anything, but it hit me with the force of a bad one-night-stand the morning after. You know the feeling you get when you wake up next to someone really ugly, or next to someone really ugly on the bathroom floor, and think, "What the fuck did I just do?" You know immediately that, what seemed to be a great idea only mere hours ago, you would now be regretting for a long time. Well, it felt just like that, but in stereo sound. I now heard what El Negro was hearing. It was like being in a loud tunnel, wherein everything is amplified and you're screaming to be heard, but you aren't really screaming over anything. All of the noise I heard was echoing inside my head. I kept telling myself that the pounding in my chest was not a heart attack and that it would stop soon. Except it didn't.

I was in the midst of this panic, yet I kept feeling the whole warm-and-fuzzy sensation, too. I kept wanting to feel things and lick things. Some people find that kind of thing fun, but I am a control freak. It took using a drug that thrives on loss of control for me to realize that I should never do anything like that again. Smoking pot doesn't bother me. I laugh, I dance, and I eat high carbohydrate foods. Even the few times I have eaten mushrooms were fun. However, I was convinced that this man-made drug consisting of god-knows-what severely fucks with the neurological chemical imbalance I already have. I was not having fun.

By this time, I was in the throes of rolling, and we were speeding down the road in El Negro's yellow Mustang with the top down. For the average person, the combination of the wind in your face, loud music, and ecstasy would make for an awesome trip. But, I felt like I was getting thrown out of an airplane with no parachute. The wind was hitting me in the face with such force that I couldn't breathe. It was like someone had duct-taped headphones to my head playing a constant loop of eardrum-busting House music. In case you hadn't noticed, I do not like House music. If raves had rock or even rap music, I might be into it. As it stands, I don't give a shit about the rise and fall of the beat and the climax of the track. It sounds like shit to me and gives me a headache. I just want to dance with the glow sticks in silence.

I asked the guys if we could just go chill somewhere for a bit, hoping I would get a grip and start enjoying myself like they were. Nope. They were headed full speed to an after-hours club sixty miles away. Hell, no! I was being driven toward my death. I begged them to take me to Katrina's house. I knew she was home, and she could calm me down—or, at least, that would be a safe place for me to hide until this synthetic, devil drug wore off. They dropped me off at Katrina's and sped off into the night. I wasn't even disappointed that I couldn't hang out with Brad and have the chance to hook up with him later. He had practically rubbed a hole in the leg of my jeans, and I was getting a bit worried when he kept talking about how awesome it would be to shoot things while rolling. Guns and ecstasy cannot be a good combination.

I was probably about a junior in college at this time, and Katrina was living in a townhouse with our friend Nate. The two of them had been drinking all day and well into the evening by the time I got there. I ran inside and locked the door, hoping the bad trip I was now experiencing wouldn't follow me inside. I entered to find Nate and Katrina on the couch surrounded by liquor bottles and watching *Dazed and Confused*. They were also in the middle of a very serious drinking game when I collapsed on the couch. I told them I thought I had taken some bad ecstasy and pleaded with them to take me to the emergency room to have my stomach pumped. It worked for alcohol poisoning, so why wouldn't it work on drugs, too? Not that I have ever had alcohol poisoning or my stomach pumped, but, at this point, I was willing to do anything to make it stop.

They looked at each other and then studied me for a few moments, when Nate said, "Well, it's time we told you." "Told me what? Oh, shit, I am going to die, aren't I?! I am going to die! I knew it! Get me some water, stat, before I dehydrate to death!" Nate tried to calm me down. "No, no you are not going to die. You're just having a bad trip. We know exactly how to make you feel better." Nate continued, "See, Katrina and I have been doing X for years. We just never told you because we didn't think you were cool with it. We're actually rolling right now". So, my two best friends were secret ecstasy users? Every time I thought they were drunk or stoned, they were really rolling on X? Now, I was really going crazy! Everything I thought I knew wasn't true anymore, and my head was spinning, and the pictures on the walls were all starting to blend together. I wanted to close my eyes, but I was afraid I would be blind when I tried to open them again.

But, I would have to deal with this new information about my friends later. They were claiming they knew all about rolling and could help me feel better, and that is all I cared about at that moment. "Fine, fine! Just tell me what to do to make it stop! I'll do anything!" Nate told me to lie upside-down on the couch with my feet in the air and head hanging off of the edge to slow my heart rate. I flipped over and waited for the feeling to subside. It wasn't working, so Katrina suggested that I dance it out. They turned on some Phish and told me to dance as hard as I could. They sat on the couch urging me on as I flailed my body around the living room, trying to stripper-shake the drugs out of my system. If there had been a pole, I could have made a lot of money with all that dancing. The only thing I had accomplished, however, was drenching myself in sweat and entertaining Katrina and Nate.

They continued to suggest that I try ridiculous thing after even more ridiculous thing. "Trust me," Katrina said, "I have bad trips all the time and this shit works. You just have to keep trying until something starts to work." I drank beer mixed with orange juice. They said the combination of alcohol and Vitamin C would take the edge off. I did yoga poses and even copied their chants that they claimed relaxed them in a moment of trippy turmoil.

I was desperate. Nothing was working and I was starting to think that I would be hallucinating for the rest of my life! Finally, Nate told me there was only one thing that he knew of that would make the roll stop, but he wasn't sure that I'd go for it.

"No, tell me! I'll do anything! I swear to God I will never take X again if you just make it stop!" Nate said, "Okay, lie down with your head tilted back on the couch again and close your eyes. Take several deep breaths in and out through your mouth." I obliged, and he started to lean over me. I braced myself for a slap in the face or a bucket of water to be thrown on me, when I heard Katrina's muffled squeals. I opened my eyes to Nate taking his pants off! "What the fuck are you doing?!" I screamed. "I was going to tea-bag you. It works every time, I promise. Just close your eyes and open your mouth."

These two fuckers that called themselves my friends had been screwing with me the whole time! They had never even done ecstasy, and this sick fratty fuck, Nate, was about to put his balls in my mouth! I had fucked with Katrina a few times myself. Was this payback for yelling "skunk" every time she walked out the door, after she had been sprayed by one a few months earlier? This was not a fair fight. I thought I was about to die from an ecstasy overdose, and these assholes were rolling on the floor laughing at me! Even though I only took one-and-a-half pills, to someone with a minor case of OCD like me that was a life-or-death situation.

I stormed upstairs and locked myself in Katrina's room. I lay on her bed and counted the revolutions the ceiling fan made for three hours until my trip stopped. It was almost 6:00 a.m., and

Sam and the guys were finally on their way back from the after-hours rave club. When I went downstairs, Katrina was asleep on the couch, the one on which I'd had my near-death experience just hours earlier. Nate was passed out on the floor. I left him a note, which I wrote on his forehead in permanent marker. It read: "I love to get tea bagged." Since Katrina was my best friend, I decided not to vandalize her. Instead, I left her a message on the whiteboard in the kitchen. "Be warned: Payback is a bitch!" She looked over her shoulder for months waiting for my revenge.

The guys had just pulled up, and they looked like they had quite an interesting experience. Sam had his shirt on inside-out, Brad had glow paint all over him, and they claimed they had lost El Negro when he tried to fight a guy for a glow stick in the middle of a foam party. I have not done ecstasy since, and I do not plan to. But, if I ever do take a hallucination-inducing drug again, I plan to lock myself in a dark room with a camelback full of Gatorade, a Snuggie, and a lava lamp.

I'm With the Band

I am oddly attracted to red-heads. Not necessarily physically attracted, but more so intrigued. There is something about that fiery feistiness that turns me on. I am naturally curious if the rest of their body hair matches what's on their head. My best friend, Katrina, is a red-head, and I even used to find myself jealous of her thick, auburn locks and perfect skin. Until, what I can only refer to as the Great Sunburn of Spring Break 2002. Katrina now only goes into the sun if she is dressed like a Muslim.

My sophomore year in college, I met a cute fraternity boy named Alan at a bonfire one night. If he hadn't had a guitar and a good voice, then I never would have given him a second look. This goes along with my philosophy on most musicians and professional athletes. Give an average-looking guy a guitar or a football, and he's sexy as hell. Give an ugly guy a number one album or an NFL contract, and he's a god. Sorry, Peyton Manning, but that is something you and Keith Richards have in common. Maybe it was the glow of the fire, or it could have been his red hair, while he sang "Brown-Eyed Girl" that had me hooked. He was my first true ginger. He didn't have strawberry-blond hair or even dark-brown-with-a–tinge-of-auburn. Alan had what could only be described as "carrot-top"! Like I said, musical ability does wonders for a guy.

I would tag along to his gigs a few nights a week. His "gigs" were pretty much singing at frat parties and hogging the microphone at local karaoke nights. He did get a gig playing with his band at a big Halloween party that everyone I knew was going to. We had been seeing each other for awhile, and I was super excited to show off my music man to my friends, and then have dirty, groupie sex later that night on top of an amp.

I love Halloween because it's the one night of the year you can dress like a total slut and get the right kind of attention. I had already done the Playboy Bunny and Sexy Construction Worker in years past. I found that the sexy version of male-dominated career costumes had the highest success rate. I also liked my costumes to be functional. One year, I was a super hero called "Beer Girl". My beer can holster came in handy since I didn't need to go to the bar for refills. But, my favorite costumes were blue-collar worker uniforms that I slutted up so much, they wouldn't even be appropriate at a bachelor party. I have done Sexy Cop, the aforementioned Sexy Construction Worker, Sexy Mechanic, and even Sexy Oil Rig Worker.

Once I had paid enough homage to the unappreciated working man with my cleavage for several Halloween's, I moved on to celebrities. I wore a bald cap and no underwear and beat people with an umbrella as Britney Spears in the Middle of a Mental Meltdown one year. I fashioned my own alcohol-monitoring ankle bracelet and popped fake, candy pills all night as Lindsay Lohan. Last year, I went all out with fake tattoos and track marks and smeared baby powder all over my face to emulate the coke-and-heroin-addicted Amy Winehouse (who was, back then, still miraculously alive, despite all her efforts to achieve the opposite).

However, this particular year I had gone back to the working man and dressed up as a Sexy Cop. My costume pretty much consisted of a navy, low-cut leotard with handcuffs and a toy gun. I used my holster to store my cigarettes, cell phone, and extra mini bottles of vodka. I went with a group of my sorority sisters to the party and was bragging about how I may not see them much since I would be backstage with the band. The party was at some rich fraternity boy's house, and he had probably spent thousands of dollars turning his parents' house into a version of *Haunted Cribs*. This was definitely going to be a great night, and the fact that I was there with the talent made me the envy of all the other wannabe groupies. Or so I thought.

I was not aware that the band would also be in costumes. Alan really should have coordinated with me or, at least, consulted me for costume approval. I walked in to see, in the center of the stage, above hundreds of people, singing a Journey song, my guy dressed as fucking Ronald Macdonald! My mouth dropped to the floor, and I turned the color of his hair in embarrassment. The bass player was even dressed as the Hamburgler! Alan couldn't have thought of anything a bit sexier than a fast food restaurant mascot? My sorority sisters asked me if the lead singer was really the guy I was dating. I could tell by the condescending tone of their voices that they were trying to do that "supportive friend, but I'm really going to make fun of you later" thing. I loved my sorority sisters, and they made my college experience anything but boring. But, any group of girls thrown together and given enough alcohol gave me terrible flashbacks of a fourth grade sleepover at which I ended up wetting the bed and returning home with new bangs, courtesy of my "mean girl" playmates.

I was desperate to crawl under the nearest rock. I had to think quickly, so I told the girls that this band must be the opening act. My new guy was probably upstairs meditating to prepare himself for his performance. He was, of course, a very serious musician. Alan had told me several times that they were turning down record deals because he didn't want the band to be too main-stream, and he wanted to stay true to the sound.

I'm not too sure what sound that was, since all they sang were other people's songs.

I decided I had to get out of there ASAP. Alan had not seen me yet, and I could just tell him I never showed up because I was sick or something. I was shoving my way back through the crowd and headed for the door when it happened. Alan, in all his red-haired, clown glory dedicated the next song to "a very special girl". I was afraid to stop and turn around, but he was already making his way off of the stage and toward me. I had been spotted, and this was not where I wanted him to make a big, romantic gesture. I'm usually all about being the center of attention and even more so when someone else is shining the spotlight on me. But, with Alan, in that get-up? A candlelit dinner alone would have done just fine.

I didn't know what to do. I panicked and went into defense mode. My defense mechanism of choice was to lie at all costs: make up whatever you have to in order to diffuse the situation as soon as possible. He had almost reached me with microphone in hand and was beginning the first verse of "Brown-Eyed Girl." I was surrounded by my confused sorority sisters, when I reached for the drink in my police holster to throw in his face. Unfortunately, the entire holster went with my "Seven and Seven". I screamed something to the effect of, "Stop calling me, you crazy stalker!" I ran out of there and never looked back. I was relieved that no one had called to interrogate me about my dramatic exit at the party. I had already prepared my damage control and was going to tell my friends that I had been trying to keep my stalker a secret, because it was just so terrifying to be stalked by a psychotic red-head, and I was too fragile to talk about it now—and probably ever.

I felt bad for what I had done, but I figured it would never work out anyway if he couldn't even choose an appropriate Halloween costume. I was trying to forget about the whole nightmare when the doorbell rang. It was Alan. He had come by to return my holster, which still contained my cell phone. I took it from him a bit ashamed and mumbled something about me having to go home to California for a few weeks to help my mother recover from a mini-face lift. He said he thought a bit of distance would be good, since I apparently had some "issues to work through." The only "issue" I had to "work through" was re-evaluating my choice in guys.

I went back inside and discovered twenty-three missed calls and seventeen text messages on my phone. They were voicemails and texts from my sorority sisters that varied from, "What the fuck was that?!" to the predictable "Are you okay?" and all the way to, "I think mixing the pot and those six Jager Bombs were probably not a good idea for you last night." The last text was from another sorority sister and it read, "I just saw some guy dressed as Ronald Macdonald doing a keg-stand while wearing your holster. Where are you?"

Girls Get Beer Goggles, Too

It happened at one of the many homecoming football games I attended in college. I had been tail-gating all day, drinking the sorority girl's cocktail of choice: Crystal Light and vodka (also known as a "White Trash Roofie", a "Roofie Colada", or the "Sorority Sauce"). I usually only needed about one-and-a-half of them, and I was the best drunk in town. I even had the pleasure of running into an ex and his new eighteen year-old girlfriend, just as I hit the peak of my buzz and was feeling overly confident. I was perfectly rude and sweet all at the same time and walked away feeling pretty damn good about myself. Until, I tripped over a stake that was holding up a tailgating tent. I then said, "Fuck it!" and killed my second Roofie Colada.

I was well into my third when a friend introduced me to a guy named Aaron. Aaron was tall and built with a sexy beard, like he hadn't had time to shave while living out in the woods, hunting animals and chopping wood and that kind of manly shit. Aaron had graduated already and used to play on the baseball team. We all know how I feel about supporting college athletics, even if you are an alumnus. I talked my friends into going to the bar I knew he would be at after the game. I did not plan on hooking up with Aaron. My only intentions were to get some much-needed male attention after embarrassing myself in front of my ex earlier (I was starting to realize that telling my ex's new girlfriend that she looked like a kid I babysat was probably not the best idea).

The fourth Roofie Colada went down too easily, and Aaron had enjoyed a few as well, hanging on my every slurred word.

> **Guys make fun of the Crystal Light and vodka and say we women only drink it to cut back on calories. That is true, but it is also a quick and easy way to get drunk. It's straight vodka with flavored sweetener. I dare any man to drink a few of those and then go try and shotgun your beer!**

I don't even remember who won the game or the name of the bar we went too afterwards, but it must have been a lot of fun based on the following events, because the night took a tumble downhill rather quickly. Aaron and I were sitting super close and flirting for all of twenty minutes when he said, "You want to drive me home and mess around"? "Sure," I said, "why the fuck not?" We got to Aaron's townhouse and wasted no time before we started making out. Before I knew it, he had whipped out about ten condoms and was at it. The sex was a bit too rough for my taste, but I figured at the pace he was going, it wouldn't last that long. Guess again. Apparently the Roofie Colada causes inability to ejaculate in men. I hadn't had anything to drink in at least an hour or so, and my happy-drunk delirium was starting to wear off fast.

We went from the bed to the dresser to the kitchen counter and even to the oversized black bean bag he had instead of a couch. I couldn't take anymore! He was literally fucking the life out of me! If only I had had more alcohol, I could have drunk some more and passed out or puked, something to make him stop. I even tried the, "Oh, wow, you're so good, I don't think I can take anymore!" This guy was not a quitter. He would not give up. I understand blue balls are a terrible thing for men, but sometimes you just have to throw in the towel. He finally took a break to re-group in the bathroom. I prayed he was jacking himself off. But, I couldn't take any chances and my vagina couldn't take any more dick, so I made a phone call.

I'll admit that I am guilty of doing the "safety net" call from a friend on a date. You know what I mean. The phone call you get from your girlfriend in the middle of a date where you can fake an emergency to bail if it sucks. In a perfect world, the date goes well and you hit ignore. In this particular situation, I had to make a plea for a safety net. I sent Katrina a text while Aaron was in the bathroom, which simply said, "Bad fuck, call and save me, say it's an emergency, now!!!!!" Just as Aaron's naked ass strolled out of the bathroom, ready for Round 7, my phone rang. "What, wait, what? An emergency, a disaster you say! I'm on my way!"

I stumbled around, searching for my clothes in pretend panic, as I explained that my friend was having some kind of catastrophe and that I had to rush to her side. I will never, ever forget as long as I live what I saw when I turned the light on to look for my bra. Aaron was sprawled lengthwise, as if he was posing for Playgirl, completely naked on that fucking black bean bag! I realized I was now sober, and he was no longer big and strong and manly. Aaron was 6'4" and tipping the scales somewhere near 300 pounds! I now understood the meaning of the movie title *Coyote Ugly* and that beer goggles was something that really did happen. I always thought that was just an excuse for bad taste.

Aaron was still naked on the black bean bag when I bolted out of there with my heels in my hand. For days, I had nightmares about being chased by an overweight baseball player wearing nothing but a baseball mitt and dragging a black bean bag. I now dilute my Crystal Light and vodkas with water.

Part Four

Back in the Saddle

Cyber Rejection

So, I'll admit it. I have tried online dating: eHarmony, Match, SugarDaddy.com—I've given them all a spin. But, here is what I've found that is so disappointing about these sites, and why they seldom work. The quality of men is terrible. Is it really that much harder for men to snag a date than it is for women? Now, I'm not female-seeking-female, but I wanted to check out my competition. And, there are some pretty attractive, well-educated, and successful women on these sites. So, who do they get to choose from? "Male in BFE TN, three kids, divorced, loves the outdoors and running", but his photo is clearly taken from within his man cave, and he is clearly sucking in his beer gut.

I don't like meeting men at bars. The only thing they want is to take you home and send you out early the next morning, promising that phone call that's never made. Life changed drastically in just a few years after college. All of my girlfriends are now in a relationship or married, and so are all of their friends. Some even have children already. I am the last eligible, single girl I know. So, with my limited resources of meeting the man of dreams, these matchmaking sites only disappointed me further with their lack of selection. Apparently, in the cyber-dating world, "quantity is better than quality". But, not for me.

Things You Don't Put in Your Online Profile

I used to believe that the couples on the eHarmony commercials were real-life couples telling their love story of how Wi-Fi brought them together. I had just gotten out of a relationship, and I was hesitant to jump back into the dating world. Well, maybe, more "lazy" than "hesitant". The idea of having to go through all the "getting to know you" bullshit and "what's your favorite song" crap made me tired just thinking about it. I wanted to roll over and go to sleep before even having sex. Never mind the foreplay. I figured that online dating was my solution. I could put all that information out there and not have to repeat it over cheap wine and overcooked filet at another poorly chosen steakhouse.

Everything there was to know about me was right there on the screen, click it or leave it. Just the basics, though. I didn't find it appropriate to put my OCD issues and family history of mental illness in an "about me" section. Saying up front that you prefer to be laid-back in a relationship, and then suddenly turn into a jealous bitch, may be moving too quick, too soon. Those things are better revealed a few months into a serious relationship, once it's too late for him to change his mind.

I tried Match.com because you can browse for men. I love shopping and I love guys, so I figured this would be a perfect marriage of the two. Well, it was, if you like shopping at the dollar store. I ditched Match and went to what seemed to be a more reputable site, eHarmony! I didn't get to browse for guys like shopping at the mall. This was more of a personal shopper experience. "Matt" and I matched on "23 out of 31 levels," except that he was soon deploying to the Middle East, and I am not so much the outdoors or waiting type. "Don" and I matched on 25 levels, accept that his other 250 matches were keeping him pretty busy. I decided to give old eHarmony one more shot and ended up with "Tripp". Tripp was a former college basketball player (check for fulfilling my fantasy of being with another college athlete!) now living in Georgia, working as a project manager (I may also have been developing a sub-conscious attraction to guys from or living in Georgia).

I have often wondered what people like project managers actually do. What kind of projects do they actually manage? Like the occupations of *The Bachelor* contestants. "Ashley is 23, from NYC and works as a fashion consultant." But, in reality, Ashley really folds t-shirts at The Gap upstate. Tripp claimed he worked on a construction site. He could just as easily have been lying and been a construction worker, or maybe he really was a project manager. But I could easily be project manager if the project consisted of Elmer's glue and construction paper. Nevertheless, Tripp and I hit it off immediately.

Our e-mails quickly transitioned to IM. We bantered back and forth with the ease of two IT techs having a forbidden office affair. We would talk for hours on the phone at night, then text or call each other first thing in the morning. We decided to meet in person, and Tripp agreed to make the six-hour drive to my house. The eHarmony guidelines tell you not to tell a date where you live or give up too much personal information on the first meeting. But, we had already had phone sex, so I was pretty sure that exempted me from those cautionary warnings.

When Tripp arrived, he was even hotter than in his pictures. It was like we had known each other for years! I was immediately comfortable with Tripp, and it was obvious neither of us were disappointed. I have been on a few too many meet-ups where the guy obviously had not updated his online profile in ten years and 100 pounds ago. Todd was just as he looked in his pictures, and we talked for hours over dinner and several glasses of wine. I wasn't planning on introducing Tripp to my friends until I had made up a believable story about how we had met. But, I was buzzed from the wine, and so proud that my online match hadn't turned out to be an overweight, balding midget, that I wanted to show him off.

Some of my friends were at a bar nearby, so I figured it couldn't hurt to stop in and have a drink and let them wonder about my hot mystery date. I rarely ever get the chance to brag or show off to my friends, mostly because I never have anything to show off or brag about. So, when I can flaunt anything that throws a bit of envy my way, then I'm all for it! I told Tripp that if anyone asked how we met to tell them we met in line at the grocery store. Every woman dreams of meeting a hot guy at the grocery store, and it was also an untraceable alibi, so that my friends couldn't question him into a corner or catch me lying.

> **A little tip to those of you that are considering introducing a guy to your friends: find out what kind of drunk he is first! Guys tend to indulge in the alcohol to relax around a group of women. Meeting your friends can be a lot of pressure, and there's no better way to relieve it than with Bud Light and Jager Bombs.**

My friends were very impressed with Tripp....at first. They thought he was funny and charming, and such the gentleman when he bought all of us a round of shots.

However, three rounds later, things started to go a little awry. Our group was enjoying yet another round of shots provided by Tripp, when an old friend approached the table to say hello. The old friend happened to be an extremely hot guy, and Tripp immediately put his arm around me to let the guy know we were together. Old, extremely hot friend wasn't coming over to flirt with me, but I did kind of like the attention I was getting from Tripp when he thought another guy might be interested in me. Most women will not admit it, but we like the feeling we get when our men are a bit jealous. When old, extremely hot friend sat down to join our group for a bit, Tripp practically pulled me into his lap. He was acting like a dog pissing all over a tree to mark its territory. When he began trying to stick his tongue down my throat in front of all my friends, I got pretty irritated. Remember, I'm not a big fan of PDA. Tripp was trying to have foreplay in a public place, and that was making me a bit uncomfortable.

I pried him away from my face and excused myself to the bathroom to smoke a cigarette and have some much needed alone time. In a crowded bar, it can take over thirty minutes to get to the bathroom and back. You have to navigate through throngs of people trying to order drinks to a bathroom that is almost always in the furthest, darkest corner of the bar. Then, you have to wait in line for who-knows-how-long to use the one stall that at least ten other women in front of you are waiting for. By the time you hover, pee, and wash your hands, the band has already come back from its break, and you *still* have to get back through the crowd.

When I finally arrived back at our table, Tripp and my friend Amanda were in deep conversation. I sat down and realized that Tripp was clearly upset about something, and she was trying to console him. Amanda is not the nurturing, "you can cry on her shoulder" type. She doesn't even like to be around you if you cry. So, the fact that she was at least pacifying a near-stranger in pain alerted the sirens in my head. I only caught the end of the conversation, but, over the band's third Journey cover, I heard Amanda say what I thought was, "You should probably get professional help for that." Oh, shit. What kind of mental and/or physical illness did this guy have? Herpes? Bi-polar disorder? Both? I was trying to have a good time, but it was clear that I needed to take control of the situation.

I asked Tripp if everything was okay. I braced myself for him to confess that he is really married or maybe has only six months to live. Nope, I couldn't get that lucky. Tripp rolls up the sleeves of his polo to reveal scars all over his arms! It looked like he had gotten in a fight with a feline in heat. Or, maybe they were kinky sex scratches? I could hang with that. I asked him what they were, and he confessed that when he gets angry, he cuts himself.

Now, I have seen enough Oprah to understand that self-mutilation is a serious disease and not something to joke about—if you are a highly emotional and depressed teenage girl. Not a twenty-five year-old male! I was speechless. I wasn't a therapist, and, after six Jager Bombs, I was even going to have trouble talking myself out of the hangover I was going to have in the morning. I tried to console him, but the tears were starting to well up in his eyes. No fucking way! This guy was not going to start crying on me! Seeing a man cry makes me extremely uncomfortable. It's on a whole other level.

Men are supposed to be tough and strong, and to shed tears—it's just unnatural and definitely not masculine. If you want to get rid of me, then shed a few tears about your hard childhood or your lack of feeling needed. It's not that I am a cold-hearted person. I care, and I'm sympathetic. But, seeing a man cry triggers a severe reaction of discomfort in me, and I literally cannot handle it!

I did the only thing I knew to do. I got Tripp another drink. I kept feeding him alcohol, until he had another mood swing and forgot about whatever it was that was about to bring him to tears (Oh, yeah, how could I forget so quickly that he was a cutter? I just nearly avoided that disaster). I finally talked him into leaving and apologized to my friends, as Tripp shoved his keys into my hand. I knew Amanda and the others were not going to let me live this one down. They still refer to him as the "that guy that cried in the bar". I drove us back to my place in his car and stopped at McDonalds on the way to get Tripp some food to soak up the alcohol. I had already decided that I wasn't going to be seeing him again, since he embarrassed himself and me in front of my friends. But, that didn't mean I wasn't going to get the poor guy a drunk, late-night snack. See, I do have a heart! The less hung over he was the next day, the quicker he would leave.

I was in the drive thru ordering at McDonalds, when Tripp leaned over me across the driver's side and started screaming, "Get me a fucking Frosty!" I explained to him that we were not at Wendy's and that there were no Frosties at McDonalds. "Order me a Frosty, bitch!" He demanded.

Have you ever been on a date that turned into such a disaster that all you could do was laugh about it? This was my date. I finally placated him with a Big Mac and an ice cream cone. Tripp had turned into a drunk, slobbering child.

We got back to my house, and he was so wasted that it took him three tries just to get inside! Each time he got a little bit further, but then would sit down in the driveway, until he finally got in the house. At this point, I have accepted the fact that, even if he was able to have sex, I have my morals and it wouldn't be right or physically satisfying. Fucking a sloppy, self-mutilating drunk goes past my moral line. Yes, even I have a line I don't cross.

Tripp dropped himself into a chair at my dining room table and went to work on his meal with the same concentration as if he were disassembling a nuclear weapon.

> ## Never try to take food away from or interrupt someone in the middle of a drunken binge.

How would you feel if someone tried to pry the Ben and Nate's away from you after a bottle of wine and a bad break-up? Not from my cold, dead hands! I went upstairs to bed alone and actually a bit relieved that I didn't have to deal with him anymore. I drifted off to sleep with hopes of a better match online next time around.

The next morning I prepared myself for the inevitable apology that Tripp owed me for his behavior last night. "He's probably down there cooking me breakfast right now to make up for his self-abuse confessions to my friends and terrible drunk ettiqette," I thought. I went downstairs to witness what could have been the best "What the fuck happened to me last night?!" scene in history. I was so stunned that I didn't even think to take a picture before I woke him up. There was Tripp, completely naked, still sitting at my dining room table, with the remnants of his Big Mac surrounding him and the ice cream cone melted all over his naked body! I tapped him on the shoulder and could barely contain my laughter when he gained consciousness.

When he asked me what had happened I decided to have a little fun. I told him that he wanted to get freaky with some food last night. I continued to tell him that things got a bit too kinky for me when he asked me to stick the ice cream cone up his ass (I love messing with someone and seeing the horror and embarrassment spread over his or her face). I told him that he had actually asked me to leave him alone to let him finish himself! Tripp put his clothes back on and had a look of shame in his eyes, like a puppy that had just shit on the floor and knew he had fucked up. Who knows what he thought he had done to himself with that ice cream cone! He was already half-way out the door when I was suggesting that he may want to seek some kind of professional help for his issues and wished him luck on his search for the right girl, since I was definitely not her.

I did take away a few things from this experience:

The only way to reason with a drunk is lie to him. Then, have some fun and fill in his blank memory with a wildly outrageous story.

Always be absolutely thorough when reading someone's online dating profile. "Social drinker" could really mean "sloppy and violent drunk".

Most of all, it's never too soon in a relationship to ask for a background check and complete mental health history.

Re-negotiating My Standards

In college, I would go for the fraternity boys with six-pack abs and pretty, baby faces. Well, I'm not in college anymore, and I definitely don't look like I did in college. So, I think it's time to re-negotiate my standards in a man. Not lower, just adjust. I don't want a twenty-three year-old that wants to take me to Chili's for "2 for 1's" before the toga party. I'm looking for a long-term thing, here. And, I know the saying about how you "learn to love someone's flaws", but there are some things I just can't get down with.

If you are over thirty and living with your parents, you need a better job or a better shrink. Maybe both. I require that you have a real job. I know bartenders and door guys are fun and can help me save money, but I don't want to date them.

I also find myself attracted to really tall guys. Like, NBA standard tall. I have lowered it by a few inches. You must be at least 5'11" to ride this ride. That way, you are still taller than me in heals. I wear the heels; you don't! On a side note, I am also not okay with even the slightest bit of "metro"-sexuality.

The height requirement also prevents me from getting an aerial view of your bald spot. It seems like men are losing their hair younger and younger these days. That's okay, I understand. The older I get, the further away I get from that tight, little body I had five years ago. But, I dress accordingly. I'm not walking around in belly shirts with low-rise jeans. Buy some Rogaine, style it differently, at least put on a fucking hat! Bald men, by choice, can be sexy. But, bald *spots* are just a reminder of what's not to come (as in, hair). As I get older, the pool of potential male suitors dwindles. So, I guess at the very least, I will cross my fingers and hope for a full head of hair.

Are You a Guy or a Man?

I refer to most males as "guys". I feel that, unless you are under ten years-old and still have John Deere tractor sheets (yes, they do exist), then you are at least a guy. But, most men I come in contact with are still just guys. Being called a "man" is a big deal and not easily attained from me. So, if you are not sure which category you fall into, the following chart should help you out:

You are a Guy if:	You are a Man if:
You use empty liquor bottles as decoration in your home.	You have real furniture like tables and chairs in your home.
You still take your laundry somewhere else to do it.	You own a suit that you wear somewhere other than to weddings and funerals.
You prefer to text over call; or even worse, Facebook!	You call someone if you want to talk. Or, even better, have a conversation face-to-face.
You take a first date to anywhere with a 2 for 1 special or peanuts on the floor.	You know how to cook.
Your friends still call you by your frat nickname.	Sometimes people call you by "Mr." followed by your last name, and you're not even in trouble.
You talk a girl into giving you a blow-job and do not reciprocate (this is just tacky and bad manners).	You know the beauty of reciprocation. I'll scratch your back, if you scratch mine.
You have a keg in your fridge.	You have anything other than beer and leftovers in your fridge.
You are a bartender, door guy, or bus boy.	You have a job where you do not live off of tips.
If you constantly refer to yourself as a man and brag about what a man you are.	Real men don't need to brag.

So, if you fall into the "man" column, then feel good about yourself. You are not an embarrassment to the male species!

If not, then call me, and I'll pretend to treat you like a man, while I really make fun of you to my friends.

Bookstore Breakdown

I had been dating this handsome home builder/realtor for a few months. He friended me on Facebook, and we went out for drinks a few days later. Honestly, I probably would not have had 75% of the relationships or sex that I've had in the last four years were it not for Facebook. Where was this when I was in college? I had MySpace then, and it certainly wasn't as reputable. You could never be sure if someone was a child molester or a transsexual. Anyway, this guy was definitely in the "man" category. He had a successful career, his own home, and had business dinners several times a week to meet with important clients. The only "business dinners" I attended were with my dad when he'd come to visit and pay for the meal with his company card! This guy had his shit so together that he was even building a home for his parents and was letting them stay with him in the meantime. Handy, manly, and good to mom and dad; I had hit the mature male jackpot!

We spent a lot of time at my house because hanging with his parents would have been weird. And, we hung out usually after 9:00 p.m., since he had all those important business dinners. I know what you're screaming: "Red flag, bitch! Abort, Abort!!" But, you must consider, I may or may not have been accused of being a bit paranoid and jealous in past relationships. So, I really wanted to be cool and mature for what *seemed* to be a real, grown-up guy. He even said how nice it was that I never questioned him because he'd had exes that were always so suspicious. So, I buried my concerns with Jack Daniels and cigarettes and went on in blissful denial.

After about three months of dating, he declared that he "has to concentrate on work and needs to slow things down." He claimed he was scared because—I shit you not, and he did say this!—he was "falling for me". I was devastated. I flew home to California for a few days to get my head and my tan together. This poor guy had been so hurt in the past that he couldn't even allow himself to love me. I was dumbfounded for days. Even the California sunshine wasn't cheering me up. On my last day, I made a quick stop at Barnes and Noble to get some reading material for the plane ride back. I was thinking something along the lines of *How to Love a High-Powered Man*, or *Helping Him Love You*.

As I entered the store, my phone rang. It was one of my best friends, Margaret, and I figured she was probably calling to see how I was doing in the throes of heartbreak. Instead, she asked if I was sitting down or near any breakables. I told her to spit it out, but I had a feeling it was about the man that I'd hoped would be my boyfriend again.

> *I never give up after the first break-up. I'm a firm believer in the "third time's a charm" rule.*

Well, I shouldn't have been surprised when Margaret told me that she'd heard from a friend-of-a-friend that my guy had a fiancé! It couldn't be true! She assured me that, after a thorough investigation, it was true. I was thinking, "Wow, we only broke up a week ago. He's already found someone else and proposed in seven days!" But, there was more! She wasn't the kind of fiancé with whom he'd fallen in love within a week. He had been with her for several years! The story was that they took a "break". Obviously, he just wanted to fuck someone else for a while, and, apparently, my Facebook profile picture and lack of mutual friends won me the prize.

I immediately hung up with Margaret and called him. And, called him, and called him. If you do not answer the phone, and I am mad, I will keep hitting redial until you do. So, it's best to just answer on the first call and get it over with. When he finally did answer, I called him every obscene name under the sun. I was so mad that I even created my own names by joining already established insults with other ones. Bet he had never been called a "douche-fuck" before! The other Barnes and Noble customers must have thought I was acting out a monologue for the *Bad Girls Club*. He continued to deny it and tell me I was delusional and that I should seek mental help. Nothing pisses me off more than someone who won't fess up when he knows he's been caught.

My tantrum had me pacing up and down the fiction aisles. Very appropriate, considering this guy had based his life off of fiction. Interesting side note: He had been chosen as one of the "most eligible singles" for his town's local newspaper a few years prior. I was pretty sure he had the article framed in his office, which was actually his friend's office. He didn't have an office or his own desk. The other finalists chosen for "most eligible" were a buck-toothed firefighter and the cross-eyed girl that worked at the Clinique counter at the only department store within thirty miles from town. We are not talking *People Magazine*'s "Most Beautiful People", here. I later found out all those business dinners were family dinners at his fiancé's house. His home that he was "letting his parents stay at" really *belonged to* his parents. He was still living at home with mom and dad! *Did I mention he was in his early-thirties?!* The dream home he was building for himself was nothing but a house of lies.

After my anger had dissolved into sobs of pain and betrayal, the sobs turned into reflection. I had gone through the whole grieving process in about ten minutes inside a bookstore. Then, I realized a few things. I have never been okay with cheating. I will not cheat on someone. If shit gets that bad, I am going to tell you I want to find someone else first. It's just good etiquette. Even worse than getting cheated on, though, is someone making you the "other woman". I had never felt dirtier in my life. Well, besides that dry hump with a hippie in a tent at Bonnaroo one year. But, at least, I wasn't the one that he put a ring on. I felt bad for his fiancé, but even worse for the next girl he would secretly stick a scarlet letter to, like a "kick me sign" on her back.

I tried to collect myself, put my shades on to hide the smeared mascara, and surveyed my surroundings. I was now standing in the self-help section. How fucking appropriate.

Three years later:

I see him in a bar, kissing a tall, blond girl. I'd had a lot to drink and decided to go introduce myself to whom I assumed was his wife. I called her by her name, Angela. She said, "No, sorry, my name is Krystal. But, nice to meet you, too." "Oh, already divorced, or just never made it to the altar," I said to him smugly. He then shoved his hand with his wedding ring on it into his pocket. Krystal and I realized what was going on at the same time. The warmth began to drain from his face.

Some douche-fucks will never learn.

Going Through the Big "D": Denial

I attended a craft fair with a friend one Saturday afternoon and found the most unfortunate woman I'd ever seen. Yes, I know you are still hung up on the craft fair thing, but these are the kinds of things you do with your friends when your body can't recover from a night of body shots like it used to, and your friend is wearing a Baby Bjorn.

Anyway, I could not take my eyes off of this woman. There she was in the most unfortunately tight jeans I've ever seen, stuffing her Size 12 ass into a 6. She wore a white belt that was just barely staying clasped around her waist and a matching white tee-shirt that did an amazing job of showing off her sausage-y arms and massive tits. She had completed this entire ensemble with brown boots and a white baseball cap, which had her frizzy ponytail pulled through the back closure and a scrunch to top it off.

My phone was in my hand before my mind had even decided to take a picture of this travesty. I hid behind the nearest airbrushed t-shirt stand (airbrush art is considered a craft in the South) and took a photo—physical proof that this poor woman has no one in her life that really cares about her. My friends may sugar-coat things for me, but they would *never* let me leave the house looking like Dog the Bounty Hunter's redneck mistress.

This woman's lack of reflective surfaces in her home got me thinking. At what point do you cross the line from "Damn, I look hot!" to being totally in denial?

I'm twenty-six as I write this. Five years ago, I had a body that would put Kim Kardashian and Megan Fox to shame. I could bounce beer tops off my ass and crush cans with my abs. Not that I had ever tried those things, but I have seen strippers do it, and I know I would dominate them. Also, not to mention my perfect pair of firm and gravitationally-blessed 32DD's. Well, then I graduated college, couldn't find a job, my mother died, and I decided to medicate with Zoloft and Chili's Molten Chocolate Cake. I would wear my dark sunglasses and proceed to order three at a time and pick them up at the car side, to go. Before I knew it, I had gained forty pounds! I mean, I knew I was being unhealthy. I knew I was gaining weight, but I never realized how big I was until my friends told me. Gee, how could those selfish bitches have let me get this far into being a fatty? Oh, that's right. They were all skinny and wanted my clothes once I could no longer fit into them.

In college, I only went to the gym to find my next boyfriend. The most cardio I got was the booty-shaking contests at the club. Which, I usually won, unless I was up against a black girl (And, that just wasn't fair. It was like putting an anorexic, sorority girl in a pie-eating contest). I ate whatever I wanted, whenever I wanted. If I wanted some fried chicken at 3:00 a.m. on my way home from the bar, by God, I was going to have it! I fucked up my metabolism, and she eventually fucked me back. Hard. Let's just say that Karma is a traitorous and vindictive bitch.

Finally, when I asked my friends if they thought I was fat, they said, "You could tone up." What that really meant was, "You are a fucking whale." I have since finally dedicated my life to getting my banging body back. If Janet Jackson can do it over and over again, so can I! I don't have nearly the amount of emotional problems or fucked up family history that she does. So, the next time your girlfriend puts a cookie in her mouth, be a good friend; ask her if her boyfriend enjoys grabbing on to those love handles she's got. She will thank you for it later.

I'll Have Your Best Merlot and a Xanax

I am the youngest of five girls. The three oldest are half-sisters from my dad's first marriage. They are quite a bit older than my full sister, Carrie, and me. We didn't all spend a lot of time together, except holidays and birthdays, when we were younger. While Carrie and I were in grade school and junior high, they were in their late twenties, snorting cocaine and trying out the new sex positions they'd read about in "*Cosmo*'s Kama Sutra". I think my mother would sit at the Thanksgiving table running statistics through her head that if my sister and I were only half-related to them, then we wouldn't end up as crazy. That hopefully her normal childhood and lack of mental illness would give us a better chance at leading somewhat stable lives.

Unfortunately, the "crazy gene" that came from my dad's side of the family was too dominant, and we all got it in one form or another. My full sister Carrie thinks she is a Kardashian. It fluctuates between Kourtney and Kim, depending on how large her ass is. She even started spelling her name with a "K" for a while. Although all her friends said it would be the best costume, she refused to dress as a Kardashian for Halloween because she thought no one would get that she was in costume, and strangers would bother her for an autograph.

The oldest of my three half-sisters, Karen, is a "Type A" missionary with a love for cats. Don't get me wrong, I love Jesus, but I can only re-gift the latest Joel Osteen book so many times. Every Christmas, she gives everyone a book that is focused on whatever she thinks his or her problem is. Last year's gift was "Choosing Forgiveness," based on her view of my tumultuous relationship with my father. For my sister Beth, it is usually the latest "Overcoming Addiction" book.

Beth is an ex-pill-popping alcoholic that has been sober for several years. Great for her, except that she's now hooked on AA and NA harder than she once was to her crack pipe come payday. She is also always concerned with my dad's health. Mostly because she doesn't want him to die before she marries her next rich husband.

At our latest family dinner, she brought him a bottle of multi-vitamins and lectured him on how he should not retire anytime soon. Her sixteen year-old son just came out of the closet, and gay men always carry some kind of chip on their shoulder about their mothers, so she can count him out for supporting her pack-a-day Marlboro habit. I accidently let the gay "cat out of the bag" in front of my young niece and nephew, when said homosexual nephew and I began discussing the Art of the Hand-Job at the dinner table one night. Whoopsie! This sent the youngest of my three half-sisters, Jennifer, into panic mode. How was I supposed to know that she was trying to shield her children from reality?

Jennifer is what you might call a "control freak". She always has to have her shit in order, and then brag about it. She would be a shoe-in for the next season of *The Real Housewives of Orange County*. She insists her two-year separation from her psycho ex-husband is only temporary. Maybe she'll get cast on *Snapped*—"When Bitter Women Attack".

One time at dinner, she told me, just like she has thousands of times before, that I needed to get off the Zoloft, get in therapy, and do something with my life. Shortly after dessert, Jennifer excused herself to the restroom. Carrie then received a text and went to the bathroom, as well. She came back and asked Beth for something. Beth reached into her purse and pulled out a pharmacy-full bag of different colored pills and handed one to Carrie to return to the bathroom with. Beth then announced to the rest of us that Jennifer was having a panic attack and needed a Xanax to get off the bathroom floor of the five star restaurant in which we were dining. We have all had panic attacks. My first came after mixing an Ambien with one too many pot brownies post-bad breakup (Don't be ashamed and call it "food poisoning").

My point is, you can't pick your family. I love mine, and I embrace all of their psychotic tendencies because they accept mine. Try not to be so hypocritical with your family. The person sitting across from you at the table might be your crazy-ass in ten years and, from where I'm sitting, we all need another glass of wine!

Floored

After five years of living together and over ten years of friendship, Katrina moved out of my condo and 500 miles away from me to live with her boyfriend. I couldn't believe my best friend was leaving me alone in this scary world of single-dom to fend for myself. Who would I have to approve my outfit choices? There would be no one to rehash my disastrous dates with over wine and cigarettes on the porch. Who would help me stumble into the house to drunkenly make ramen noodles after a night out? There were so many things I was going to miss about us living together.

Except one: her little Pomeranian, Lucy. I love dogs. I have one of my own. Artie and Lucy were even best friends, too. Artie, however, did not use my bedroom carpet as a toilet. I figured if I ever wanted to find another roommate, I would have to get rid of the piss-stained carpet in Katrina's old bedroom. I hate to speak badly of little Lucy, because I love her dearly, so I won't blame the destruction of my Berber carpet on her. It could have very well been one of the drunk dials we brought home looking for the bathroom.

Once Katrina had left to co-habitate with her man, I began to search for someone to replace the carpet. Home improvements are fucking expensive! Home Depot wasn't even in my budget. So, I went to the internet's version of classifieds, Craigslist. Craigslist is the only place on the web where you can find a job, a nanny, used tires, and a prostitute in one place (This supports my theory that Craigslist was really created by some very internet-savvy prison inmates). I searched services for carpet and called the first one on the list that didn't "habla Español."

I didn't bother to background-check the guy or check him out with the Better Business Bureau.

He said he could have the job done in one day, and that was worth the risk of potential robbery or rape to me. I hate having people in my home for long periods of time. When friends come over for dinner, I'm washing the dishes during dessert, trying to hint around that it's time for them to get the hell out. My carpet guy of choice just had to come by and measure the room and let me choose what kind of carpet I wanted first.

Carpet guy showed up the next morning, and I almost had an orgasm when I opened the door. Holy Hotness! He was a blond version of Channing Tatum in *Step Up*, just less thuggish and more "ruggish". I was fully expecting an overweight, toothless handyman wearing overalls. I had hit the Craigslist jackpot! I couldn't take my eyes off of him. I was barely paying attention to the Berber samples he was showing me, as I pictured him giving me rug burns on the carpet right then and there. He even took my hand and ran it over the samples so I could get the feel of them. I just about broke into a sweat, and that's when I saw his wedding ring. Of course a guy that sexy was married!

I may not have the best morals, but cheating is one line I will not cross. I won't cheat on someone, and I won't be the one with whom someone cheats. I've learned that both of those positions are worse than being in missionary with a line backer. But, fantasizing isn't cheating, and paying him to lay my carpet wasn't illegal either. Unless, we did mess around, then that might fall under prostitution.

So, I hired him on the spot. When he returned a few days later to start the job, I made sure I had makeup on and done my hair. I wasn't going to be caught off-guard in my sweats next time the door bell rang (You never know how hot the UPS guy may be). Carpet guy did not do the best job in the world. The carpet was bulging and fraying in a few places, but that just meant he had to stay longer to fix them. He even chipped some paint on the wall while moving some furniture, which he offered to come and fix the next day. The more this guy sucked at his job, the longer I got to look at him!

He returned the next morning with some paint to repair the wall. It didn't take him five minutes to do, and he asked if he could "touch up anything else for me". I could think of a few things he could "touch"! I wondered if he thought it would be weird if I asked him to fix my squeaky mattress. I decided that may be a bit too forward and instead found every mark on every surface of my house that could possibly be re-painted. I even chipped off a little paint myself, when he wasn't looking. After a few weeks and several hot dreams involving the carpet guy and a steam cleaner, I noticed the grout breaking apart in my bathroom tiles. Hallelujah! Carpet guy did tile, too! He was actually a flooring extraordinaire. Well, he wasn't quite an extraordinaire; I actually could have done just as good of a job after a few DIY seminars at Home Depot. But, anything he charged was worth it to watch him bend over and lay that tile.

Since the new tile was a slightly different color than the old tile, and I knew my OCD would keep me up at night thinking about it, I decided to re-tile all three bathrooms! Carpet guy was at my house every day for a week! He probably felt sorry for me thinking I was some lonely rich girl with no job and no friends, because I was always there watching him as he worked. I didn't really give a shit what he thought. He was married and got to go home to his lucky-ass wife, so the least he could do was provide some fantasy material for me.

A few months later, after another disappointing break-up with my latest fling, I decided that I could not have two different kinds of carpet in the house. So, carpet guy came back to do the whole place! He was even hotter than before. It was summer time, and he was all tanned and tone. Could carpet guy also be a construction worker, too? I could bulldoze the whole damn house down and hire him for the re-build! The fact that he probably wasn't any better at building a house than he was at laying carpet meant I could keep him around for years repairing all the things he fucked up. Maybe, by that time, he would realize his love for me and leave his wife. Or, at the very least, I could catch him unexpectedly in the back of a closet and pretend I was looking for my vacuum.

When there wasn't anything else I could destroy for carpet guy to repair in my home, I had to let him go. I knew that eventually I would have to call him to come back to fix his shitty carpet and tile jobs. My friends didn't even want me to refer him because they saw his work and had someone better. I had wanted to help the guy out and get him some business, but at least I could keep him to myself now. I needed a frequent customer punch-card. Ten home repairs, and he goes down on me for free! I actually missed carpet guy after not seeing him for a while. But, alas, home improvements are expensive, so I would just have to "Facebook stalk" him until I could afford new hardwood floors.

You Might be a Hooker If

After all the home improvements were done, I found myself alone again. I went into a panic when Katrina moved out. I had not lived alone in five years. I did not want a new best friend or even someone to keep me company, just a body downstairs to make me feel not so alone in my house (Home intruders are also more likely to assault a downstairs occupant before going upstairs). The extra cash each month didn't hurt, either. My friend Will suggested a mutual friend of ours to move in with me. She actually dated my friend Nate in college, and she would come and go over the years, hanging out for a few weeks and then disappearing again. She also happened to be a clean freak, like me, who was an excellent cook, not like me. Perfect, I thought. This girl would work out nicely. She moved in and we hit it off immediately.

Within weeks, the new roomie and I were inviting my friends over for dinner parties and wine nights. She got along great with my friends, and we were all one big happy family. After a few months, though, roomie wasn't coming home every night. I didn't really care, as long as her rent checks were clearing. She eagerly told me she was seeing this guy from out of town. When he would come in for work, she would go stay with him at his hotel. She gushed about how he spoiled her and took her shopping, and that he even insisted on buying her new tires for her car. Now, I'm not a genius or a mathematician, but, when you go to a hotel with a guy and come out with cash to go shopping, that equals a business deal. And that might make you similar to a prostitute.

I made comments that he may or may not be treating her like a hooker. She passively brushed off my concerns but jokingly referred to

him as "sugar daddy" anyways. After a few more
months, sugar daddy began to be referred to by his
real name. The one his wife at home called him. I
tried to act surprised when I found out he was
married with kids. But, give me a fucking break!
The dude was bald and pushing forty. What else
could he have been but married? Things eventually
ended between the roomie and sugar daddy, at
which point I once again tried to act surprised and
sympathetic. Sympathy is not my thing. I am not a
nurturer. You want to trash-talk someone? Do
some man-bashing? I'm your girl. But, if you are
looking for someone to hold you while you cry and
wipe your tears, then you need to call your mother.

Roomie started spending more and more
time with my friends. The male friends, in
particular. Granted, she did date Nate years ago
and was sort of friendly with the rest of them
before she moved in with me, but this was getting
a bit excessive. She was cleaning their houses for
them and making them dinner several nights a
week. Of course, roomie never thought twice about
not helping me when I was on my hands and knees
cleaning the floors at our house. But, then again,
she was probably tired from being on her knees,
sucking everyone else's dicks all day. It wasn't long
before she was hooking up with these mutual male
friends, too. I had interests elsewhere, so I was not
jealous. It was just a little weird that one day she'd
liked so-and-so and brought him home, and, then,
the next night she'd spend at another one's house.
She was a lover of all men and did not
discriminate. I personally can't get down with a
married guy one week and a twenty-three year-old
the next. I prefer a bit more consistency.

Now, I know I am no saint. I sometimes
have questionable morals and do some sketchy
things. I have been called many names in my life,
but "fake" has never been one of them. Fake people

are my pet peeve. You may be a pill-popping, welfare-collecting slut, and that's your business. If you own it, then more power to you. I'm a bitch. I can be mean and lose my temper. I tell it like it is, and I love myself even more for it. So, when someone living in my home tries to tell me they are my friend but goes and fucks all my other friends, that puts me a bit on edge. The worst part was that she didn't think she was doing anything wrong! What roomie does is her business. I'm all about privacy. But, when your "privacy" starts sleeping on my couch or waking me up with its sex noises, we have a problem.

I don't blame my guy friends. They are men. A woman offers to make them dinner, do their dishes, and hook up with them? I have not met a man that can resist that. They love to be mothered, and she was a pro at using that to her advantage. I tried not to let it bother me. I tried to keep my opinions to myself. If you know me, then you understand that this is a feat I rarely accomplish. So, instead of losing my temper, I resorted to the occasional, passive-aggressive comment. These little digs would give me days of satisfaction. Roomie would say, "I'm having a wine night tonight, want to join?" I would say, "No, thanks, someone already bought all the jumbo bottles of merlot at Macaroni Grill. Oh, sorry, I didn't know those were yours."

After co-habituating for almost ten months, I had to ask her to leave (I was really sick with the stomach flu, and she refused to get me some Pedialyte). I know this is trivial and petty, but I was on my fucking death bed! She was already late for work, which she rarely showed up to at all, so I couldn't understand why she couldn't bring me some damn electrolytes to save my life. It was the straw that broke this bitch's back. I realized my worst nightmare was living downstairs. I was scared I could turn out like her one day. If I couldn't live with a thirty year-old, single, self-absorbed, two-faced lush, then I definitely did not want to become one. And I was about just one night stand and a bad hangover away from just that. I needed to purge everything bad in my life and I started with the roomie.

I tried to be civil about it and give her thirty days notice. Maybe breaking the news to her via text was bad form, but, at the time, I was still too sick to have a long, drawn-out conversation about it. I was still a bit bitter about not getting my Pedialyte too. Of course, in true lush roomie form, she over-dramatically packed all her things the very next day and left. I breathed a sigh of relief as I walked through my kitchen naked for the first time in months. I was reveling in my re-claimed privacy, when I saw her final "fuck you." Roomie had left three, empty jumbo bottles of merlot in the trash can when she knew damn good and well that glass does not go in the trash compactor. I could not accept her getting the last, passive-aggressive word.

So, I sold the hydrocodone pills I found that were left on the floor of her old bedroom and wrote this story.

I heard she had moved into another friend's house and was telling people that I didn't have any friends. One thing I learned from roomie is that, if you have to cook them dinner, do their laundry, and suck their dicks, they probably aren't really your friends.

How Permanent Is That?

I have never been the self-mutilation type. Going on a date with a cutter scarred me for life. I wasn't even into the artistic kind of scarring your body. I did have my belly button pierced when I was seventeen but almost passed out twice. I saw my sister tattoo a guy's name on her back and vowed I would never profess my love any more permanently than doodling on a crappy notebook in math class. I am always cautious of the fallout. I want to be sure that, if I change my mind and don't like something, I can get rid of it. If I break up with a guy, I immediately purge everything from that relationship. Out of sight, out of mind.

I did think the low hip and lower back tattoos were cute and sexy, until the term "tramp stamp" was coined. Until you have seen a seventy year-old woman wearing a lace thong with a butterfly or dolphin tattoo on her lower back bend over in front of you at the grocery store, you may think they are cute, too. They aren't. What is that tattoo going to look like in twenty years when it's faded and covered by stretch marks and cellulite? Not so hot now, huh?

But, I still wanted something to show a bit of my rebellious side. I cried when my mom took me to get my ears pierced as a little girl. I ran screaming out of the store and wore clip-on earrings until I was thirteen and couldn't take the scrutiny anymore. So, when I saw Lindsey Lohan rocking a tattoo done with white ink on her wrist, I was intrigued. This was before she was a lesbian and went to rehab the second time. She was still a trend-setter, having only been to rehab once. I decided to jump on the band wagon before it was too full and went to my local tattoo shop. I had the word "breathe" tattooed on the inside of my left wrist. I chose the word "breathe" because it was cool enough for Lindsey, and I could make up all kinds of stories about the deep, emotional meaning it had to me. Yes, I copied a tattoo from Lindsey Lohan. I should have known that it could be an identifying mark in a police lineup one day and that I may not want to tie myself to a person like that.

I thought a tiny little tattoo on my wrist couldn't hurt that bad. I was wrong. It hurt like a rubber band-snapping, needle-injecting bitch. The thing about tattoos is that, once you start, you can't back out. I couldn't walk around with half a word on my wrist. After it was over, I felt rebellious and tough. My tattoo was pretty damn cool. It was inconspicuous and looked almost like a brand. The pain had obviously caused amnesia about how bad it actually did hurt, and I decided it wouldn't be a bad idea to get another tattoo someday.

"Someday" came sooner than anticipated. Just a few short months later, I met a guy named James that would have put Tommy Lee to shame with all his body art. He had his arms and back completely covered in ink. In the past, I had only found tattoos sexy on musicians. But, all of James' tattoos were pretty damn sexy, too. Underneath the red flames, golden horseshoes, tribal bands, and names of what could have been several family members or illegitimate children, I found a sweet, sensitive, tough guy. James was the perfect mix of salty and sweet. He seemed like the type that would punch someone in the face for looking at me the wrong way, and then help an old woman across the street five minutes later. I gave him my number, and he called a few days later.

The night I had met him, he mentioned wanting to get a tattoo on his back colored in but didn't know a good place, since he had just moved to town. So, instead of acting like a normal female and waiting for a guy to ask me out, I asked him. If

I could find the patience to wait for a guy to call me, I probably wouldn't have enough dating disasters to write a book! Unfortunately, I like to learn things the hard way, usually repeatedly. So, I texted Josh and said that I am going to get a new tattoo and invite him to join me to get his done, too. How romantic—a date at the tattoo parlor. I couldn't have started with discussing basic likes and dislikes over dinner first? Of course not. I wouldn't be me if I didn't jump head first without looking for water. I didn't think my plan through enough to decide what kind of tattoo I wanted or even that I may actually have to get a tattoo!

James and I went to the same tattoo parlor I had gone too before. I walked in like I was some kind of regular, and we were greeted by a girl behind a desk that was covered in barbed wire. She had some kind of scrolls tattooed on her face and a nose ring that had a chain connecting to what I hoped was her nipple, and not something further down her fishnet dress. I had already decided that getting my initials, which I also share with my late mother, would be something small and cute, without being "Mickey Mouse on your shoulder" cute. I was torn on the placement. My foot could be a good place. Something not too many people would see except in warmer months. Easily hidden. Then, the back of my neck wasn't a bad idea either. My hair would cover it. My whole idea of tattoos is that they are a fun surprise if placed correctly. You think I'm nice and sweet, but, hello! There's a music note tattooed behind my ear that makes me seem deep and unstable in an "emo" kind of way! When I couldn't decide, I let James pick. He said that neck tattoos were sexy on girls. I threw my hair on top of my head, sat down, and braced myself.

It really didn't hurt as bad as my first tattoo. Now, I had a permanent souvenir and an awesome story to tell our kids about our first date. However, just like most of my plans, it didn't turn out that way. James turned out to be jacked up on Xenadrine all the time, and we stopped talking after a few weeks.

I was in a wedding a few months later and was about to walk down the aisle, when the bride sent her mother over to ask me if I could put my hair down. "Why?" I asked. The mother of the bride told me that the tattoo on my neck was showing and it "looked a hair trashy"! I turned to check out my back in a mirror and, as much as I hate to admit it, she was right. There, in between my sophisticated French twist and strapless lilac dress was the proof of a bad decision.

I still told the bride and her mom to kiss my ass and rocked my tattoo all night long. That's just me. Even if I think it's a bad idea, no one can tell me it is. It's my mistake, and I'm going to own it until there is more advancement in laser tattoo removal.

He's Not Going To Call

If He Says	He Really Means
"I'll call you when I'm done."	When I'm done curing cancer, so don't wait for my call.
"I'll call you when I get back from (insert whatever the reason he gives for not taking you out)."	From traveling to outer space to service the Russian space station. Don't wait up.
"I'll call you when I get home."	I'm homeless, so don't hold your breath.
"I'll call you right back."	Get a good book, 'cause it's going to be a while.
"I'll call you soon."	As soon as I remember your name, so you don't figure out that you are programmed as "big tits girl from bar" in my phone.

And, then he'll—nope, this guy is never going to call. Stop waiting by the phone. No answer *is* your answer.

How Desperate Am I Willing To Get?

I was in a sporting goods store shopping for a Christmas present for my niece. Not that she is a huge tomboy, but she likes to play sports. Judging from our side of the family, it is a miracle she has any athletic ability at all. The most common role my sister and I took in organized team sports was ducking and shielding our faces from the ball. I was terrified of getting hit with any sort of ball. I still am, just a different kind of ball.

However, any time I get the excuse to go to a sporting goods store or a Home Depot, I take it! Everyone knows that those places are crawling with good-looking guys. If you can talk football or dry wall, then you're already the best deal he's seen in the store.

I was comparing soccer balls when a cute guy passed by me and made some serious eye contact. I had just left the gym, and I was in sweats with no makeup and looked like shit. His nice, warm smile was probably a pity smile that really said, "You need to take your ass to the outerwear section and get a new fleece jacket, because that's all that is going to be keeping you warm at night." Nice to know there are still guys out there willing to throw a bone your way when you are not on your A-game.

I was turning the corner to head toward said outerwear section and literally ran into the same warm smile, cute guy. I said, "Excuse me," and started to continue on my way, when he asked me what I thought of the toboggan he was trying on. I said it looked nice, and he proceeded to ask me my opinion on some more headwear options. His not-so-cute friend apologized for Warm Smile, and I shrugged it off. But, Warm Smile followed me to outerwear and tried to suggest some nice options.

It was apparent that he was flirting with me. I didn't know why, because I wouldn't flirt with myself looking the way I did right then.

I went to pay, and he stood next to me in line for the register. We exchanged some serious eye contact and more warm smiles while we both waited. My ability to read lips came in handy when he not-so-quietly asked his friend if he should go talk to me again. I assumed he was trying to devise a plan to get my number. But, not-so-cute friend was shaking his head in a not-so-encouraging way.

Sorry if I'm not your type, buddy, but I obviously am for your friend, so don't be such a cock block! What happened to guys being good wingmen? I think men can be more jealous than women when it comes to their friends. A guy meets a girl and all of a sudden their friends start acting like little girls, saying "we never watch the game together anymore, man" and stupid guy shit like that. Hey, not-so-cute friend, I have some not-so-cute friends of my own that may go for you; so, again, don't be such a cock block!

I caught Warm Smile checking me out several more times, until he paid for his toboggan and left the store with his friend. I paid for my soccer ball, thinking what could have been if Warm Smile's dumb-ass friend hadn't been there. He probably would have had some balls of his own to come ask me for my number. As I was walking to my car, a truck drove past me, and Warm Smile waved at me from the passenger seat! He looked like he wanted to stop and say something, but, of course, his not-so-cute friend wouldn't slow down enough for me to even catch his name. That could have been my future ex-boyfriend, and I may never see him again!

I know what you are thinking. He was probably just being nice. Maybe, he had a girlfriend and his friend was trying to keep him out of trouble. I say, who gives a shit! There was definitely something there, and now I'm left wondering what could have been. So, this leads me to the question: What now? Do I forget about warm Smile all together? Or, do I do something proactive?

But here lies the problem. Any kind of action I could possibly take could make me look desperate and crazy. I could Facebook search him by the company name on the truck he was in. But then, what if I do find him? "Hi, I'm the broke-down-looking girl from the sporting goods store and, after some serious Facebook stalking, I hope you decide to friend me, and we can live happily ever after!" Uh, no. If I was on the receiving end of that message, I would report that person, and then make fun of him with my girlfriends. We learned how that one could turn out with the mechanic.

I have seen the "missed connections" forum on Craigslist, but does anybody ever even respond to those posts, besides sex predators and serial killers? Do I really want to go out with a guy that is sitting in front of his computer all day, hoping someone is looking for him?

> **If he were to track me down, then that would be romantic and a great story for the grandkids. But, because I am a woman and anything I may do that is a bit out of the ordinary automatically labels me a "psycho stalker". Guys will take any chance to label you as crazy. You breathe the wrong way, and he says, "What, now you're mad at me? Are you going to go all crazy on me and shit now?"**

So, what would you do? How far are you willing to go and possibly risk your pride for something that may or may not be? I decided not to take any action and just daydream of what could have been. I don't have a lot of shame, but I'd like to keep the little I do have left healthy and intact. But, I did hope that Warm Smile got my license plate number, had a good friend at the DMV, and maybe was a bit crazy, too.

Déjà Vu Date

have only ever been set up on one blind date. I have set myself up on plenty, but my friends don't usually try to set me up with complete strangers because they don't want to be blamed for my possible bad behavior. But, one of my friends told me all about this guy she thought I would hit it off with. She told me he was nice, cute, funny, owned his own business, and we even went to the same college. She showed me some pictures of him from her Facebook, since he didn't have a page, and, by the high-resolution on the iPhone 4, he definitely passed the background check. He was cute.

My future date had a nice smile and brown hair that offset the up-to-no-good look in his eyes. Just the kind I like, and also similar to the majority of Southern guys. It was only a headshot, but I could guess that he was holding an old fraternity koozi in one hand and the keys to his Silverado in the other.

I prepared for my peripheral vision-impaired date with excitement and anticipation. The doorbell rang, and I saw a tall, dark, well-built figure through my glass door. If you can judge looks by a dark shadow and not risk getting burglarized or abducted, then this guy was already ahead of the game. He was just as cute as his pictures, yet oddly familiar. He looked like most of the guys I knew in college, but about seven-to-ten years older. I didn't think too much of it. He was nice and polite and even opened the door to his— yep, you guessed it—Chevy Silverado truck for me.

We made the usual how-do-you-know-so-and-so-that-set-us-up chat on the way to the restaurant, and it hit me. That voice. I knew that voice! It was a soft, smooth Southern drawl that only makes girls that are not from the South swoon. To people in the South, he probably sounds normal. Being from Southern California, people often confuse my accent with being a Yankee. Then they get offended when I correct them and subtly mention that the Civil War was over centuries ago, and it's time to let the whole Yankee/Rebel thing go.

This guy still seemed so familiar to me! I wanted to confuse the sensation with "love at first sight", "I feel like I have known you my whole life!" familiarity, but that wasn't it. It was more of the "smoky bar, too many Jager bombs, where did I sleep last night?" familiar.

There are currently 60,000 students at the college I went to. There were about 50,000 when I was in attendance. When you were a social rock star like I was in college, you cannot be expected to remember every name and face. I didn't want to sound like a slut and ask, "Hey, have we hooked up before?" So, I started asking some strategic questions. I found out that he indeed was in a fraternity around the same time I was in a sorority. We did frequent the same bars in college and knew some of the same people. He must have sensed me checking off his answers in my head, because he finally said what I was dying to say. "We know each other from somewhere, don't we?"

After some mathematical calculations and a round of "where were you around this time in 2003?" we both stopped silent. It all flooded back like the day after a black-out drunken night. It was October, maybe November 2003. My sorority had a mixer with his fraternity. After too much alcohol and my designated driver leaving me, he offered me a ride home. At some point during that ride, I ended up at his fraternity house and in his room. All I remembered eight years later was that he had some sort of reptile as a pet. He informed me that it was his iguana Reggie that sadly passed in 2005.

Either way, we hooked up that night in 2003. We didn't have sex, but we may have had his roommate not barged in with another girl and a beer bong. I remembered it as one of those fun nights with a fun guy I didn't want to ruin with all the "what now?" crap. We didn't make any half-hearted promises to see each other again or even exchange numbers. I never saw him again and never really thought about it again, either. Until last night, eight years later, when he showed up at my door!

It turns out that he graduated that December after our encounter. Then, he moved home a few hours away from here before returning a few years later. Like most fraternity guys, he went by a nickname back then, so that explains why I didn't recognize him by name when our mutual acquaintance set us up. There really wasn't a good excuse why he didn't remember my name. I introduced myself to him using my first and last name throughout the course of the evening, just to give him a hard time. All in all, it was a nice date and a crazy coincidence.

No sparks, probably wouldn't be a second date. It did, though, give me a damn good story to write about and a lesson learned. Not every moment is meant to be memorable, but maybe some are meant to be just a fun memory. We ended the date with one promise, though. That if we do meet again in another eight years, we will remember each other's names!

The One Who Put Up With My Shit

My longest and most serious relationship was for three years with a guy named Jake. Contrary to popular belief, I really am more of a relationship person. I prefer to be half of a whole, to have a companion. My problem is I tend to rush things and want to make someone my boyfriend after date two.

We met at a bar one night in January shortly after my twenty-first birthday. I wasn't intending to meet anyone that night. I hadn't been twenty-one for long and, on this particular night, I was just excited that I didn't have to sneak my drinks to the bathroom to hide from the cops anymore. I was with Katrina, and we spotted them. Twins! Two, identical-looking, extremely hot guys, and I could tell them my real name and not the one on my fake ID! This was heaven! They did look very much alike, but I didn't think *too* identical. I was pretty sure if I didn't drink too much, then I could easily tell them apart.

Katrina was already drunk when I told her I was going to go talk to the cute one. She had no idea which one that was, so I pointed her in the direction of his brother. I headed in the opposite direction of where this guy in the blue polo was headed upon leaving the group that included his twin to sit in a booth alone. But, Katrina never even made it over to talk to his twin brother. As she was walking across the bar to approach him and hopefully persuade him into buying her a drink, she became distracted by a guy she had hooked up with the semester before and aborted her mission.

That was when my life changed forever, and I met Jake. I can't even remember what I opened with, or how I approached him. As I sat across from him in the booth, we talked about the usual, where we were from, what we studied in school, blah, blah, blah. Nothing too exciting, but there was something about him that kept my ass planted in that booth and never wanted to leave. We had been talking for a long time when Katrina came up to us, introduced herself, and then excused herself to leave with last semester's conquest (We did this pretty often with each other. Even if one of us didn't actually leave the other, we would pretend to so the guy we were talking too would have to drive us home).

It was a pretty quiet drive, and I still think about it when I hear the same country song that was playing on the radio that night as Jake reluctantly drove me home. He even more reluctantly programmed my number in his phone. If you ever have to ask if a guy wants your number, then he probably doesn't. I didn't hear from him again. I was pretty bothered by this and hoped that I would run into him again. A few weeks had gone by, and Katrina and I were out again at another bar in town when I spotted Jake playing pool. I decided that I would give him one more shot to respond to my aggressiveness (I still am not able to just let a guy come to me. I am too impatient and I don't care who gets it done as long as it gets done).

I put on some lip-gloss, pushed my boobs up, and sauntered over to him. When I asked why he never called, he replied with the lame-ass excuse of "my phone broke". Jake was acting pretty cocky, but he still seemed slightly interested, so I forged ahead (I am still not good at taking a hint either. If I was, I probably would have walked away right then, because this guy wasn't really into me at all). In this case, blind ambition worked in my favor. I happened to be driving my dad's new Hummer SUV, and Jake could not pass up the chance to drive me home in it.

He came in and we talked a bit more, and then he had a friend pick him up. That was it. I was hooked. He hadn't even acted like he liked me. But, it was too late. He was going to fall for me just like I was for him. Jake was different, though. He didn't necessarily respond to my aggressiveness, but he definitely didn't let it scare him away. I really, really liked this guy.

Even though I asked him out on our first date, and I was the one that asked him to make a commitment, he was still down with all of it. Jake either really did like me or was certifiably insane. It's one thing to put up with a girl's insecurities and craziness if she looks like Megan Fox or is giving it to you all the time, but I was fulfilling neither of those scenarios. He was the one that made me wait several long months to have sex. Did he do that because he was such a good guy? I hope so, but he's still a guy after all. I think he made me wait so long because he wanted to be absolutely, 100% sure that he really liked me before we had sex.

Jake knew me well enough at this point that he understood, once we did sleep together, he would have had a better chance breaking out of prison than breaking up with me. I still, to this day, have no idea why a guy like him wanted to be with a girl like me. He seemed perfect. He was 6'4", had sky blue eyes, a body like an Olympic volleyball player, and a smile that made old women flustered.

Well, be careful what you wish for because, as time progressed, I got really insecure about myself and our relationship. Every time we went out, I was convinced that other girls were wondering, "Why is he with her" or "He could do way better". Those insecurities, coupled with his crazy ex-girlfriend and my mom's death, made me start eating out of spite. I didn't get fat, but it was more like the movie star dating the pudgy makeup girl. Jake continued to put up with my shit. I would start fights just to test him, to see how far I could push him until he had enough. I would kick him out, or he would storm out, and I was always the one that would call crying begging him to come back. No matter whose fault it was.

Ninety-nine percent of the time I was the instigator. I started fights because I wanted more attention. I wanted more attention because I was so unhappy with myself. I had become the crazy, nagging girlfriend I dreaded. I even refused to speak to him for two whole days because he wore winter weight dress pants before Labor Day.

We still decided to move in together, which ended up being a huge mistake. My OCD was too far out of control at this time to share the same living space with someone. Even a towel on the floor sent me into a rage. It wasn't just about the towels, though. Even just the few short years of dating in college before I had met Jake made me a disaster of a girlfriend. Every other guy I had been with left me in such a disastrous way, or they did something that sent me running in terror, that I was always aware of the eventual expiration date.

I definitely was not scared of commitment. It was the opposite. I was afraid of not having it. I was terrified that one day Jake would wake up, roll over to look at me, and scream, "What the *fuck* am I doing?!" I wanted to push him so far that he would either make a huge gesture of love, so that I would never be scared of him leaving me again, or I wanted to ruin what we had myself so I wouldn't be the one getting left. I thought it wouldn't hurt as bad as long as I stayed in control and it was on my terms. He never did, though.

In the last few months that we were together, I started to shut down. I was so tired of fighting that I just didn't care anymore. I didn't want to be with anyone else, but I wasn't happy with the person I became. I was holding on so tight to our relationship that I was really pushing it away. I probably kicked Jake out at least four times before the last time. Each time, he would pack his stuff or I would throw it out on the lawn. Throwing someone's shit out on the lawn or over a balcony looks fun in movies, but the mess I was making caused me anxiety, because I knew that I wanted him to just bring it all back in. Sometimes I even packed and then unpacked his things for him! There were nights he hadn't even made it back to his house yet before I would call and beg him to come back, swearing I would stay on my meds regularly or go back to therapy.

The final time wasn't anything very dramatic or romantic comedy-worthy. Although he did threaten to piss in my shampoo bottle, which I threw away just to be safe. I kicked him out so many times that I wasn't even sure it would stick this time. But, that night, I didn't call him begging him to forgive me and to come back. I didn't call the next morning or the day after that either. One day of not calling turned in two, then three, and then a week had passed. I was almost in a little competition with myself to see how long I could go. I was not fooling myself thinking that he would call. I had called Jake many names in our three years together, but "sucker" was never one of them. I knew he wasn't going to call, because he knew he didn't have to. Eventually I would. I always did. Except this time I didn't.

After about ten days, he did call. I think that part of him thought that the only explanation for me not calling him and groveling for his forgiveness yet was that I had been abducted or was dead. The conversation was pretty simple. "Yes, I'm okay. No I have not tried to kill myself. Yes, I guess we are broken up. Yes, I'll drop off your protein shakes at your parent's house." We were both exhausted. I was tired of giving him shit all the time, and he was tired of taking it.

I have tried to get back together with him several times since then. We would talk for a day or two, maybe see each other a few times, and then I would get scared that he would change his mind and that he wouldn't want to work things out. The thought of living in that fear of him not wanting to be with me was too much. Even though I was the one that created that fear for myself. So, I would start another fight and tell him to forget the whole thing.

He must have thought I was a certifiable bitch. Maybe I was. I never stopped loving him and the possibility of not receiving that love back made me ruin things over and over again. It says a lot about a person that would even continue to answer the phone to someone like me. It took me a while to realize that Jake wasn't the bad guy in our story. Neither of us was.

I have always been my own worst enemy, and, sometimes, other people fall victim to my craziness, too. Moral of the story: If you are lucky enough to find someone that will love you and accept you for who you are and put up with all of your shit (and you feel the same way for them) that **does not mean you should bury them in it**.

> **But, until I find that person again, I am going to keep getting back on that horse called "Dating", no matter how often she keeps throwing me off.**

About the Author

Stephanie Goldman grew up the youngest of five girls in affluent Orange County, California. By the time she graduated high school, she had moved to Tennessee to attend college and fallen deeply in love with competing Tennessee Walking Horses. Stephanie also loved fashion and design, so after receiving a Bachelor of Science Degree in Fashion, she decided to stay in Tennessee and combine her two greatest loves by starting her own equestrian apparel business, CJ Jeans Co.

Stephanie would entertain her friends with stories of growing up in an unconventional household, which could have been ripped straight from a script from an *O.C.* episode. She loves making people laugh and has endless stories about college and relationships. Her sarcasm and tell-it-like-it-is writing style pulls readers into her world with ease. Because of this, Stephanie started a blog, "Did I Really Do My Hair for This?" She knew she wasn't the only twenty-something out there carrying around a magnet for disaster, and judging from the readers who visit her blog every day, she is not alone in experiencing the sort of dating disasters and awkward encounters with men that most people are too embarrassed to mention in public. Hence, her blog took off quickly and has provided many nights of laughter and fun for women all across America. Now with the release of her first book, which shares the same title as her blog, Stephanie will be putting forth her misadventures with men into print form for the whole world to enjoy.

Ms. Goldman lives just outside of Nashville, Tennessee, where she continues to search for Mr. Right.